Know The Score Books Limited

118 Alcester Road
Studley, Warwickshire, B80 7NT
Tel: 01527 454482   Fax: 01527 452183
info@knowthescorebooks.com
www.knowthescorebooks.com

A CIP catalogue record is available for this book
from the British Library

ISBN: 978-1-905449-33-0

Jacket Design by Lisa David

Book Designed by Andy Searle

Edited by Simon Lowe & Andy Searle

Printed and bound by The Cromwell Press, Trowbridge, Wiltshire

Mixed Sources
Product group from well-managed
forests and other controlled sources
www.fsc.org Cert no. TT-COC-2082
© 1996 Forest Stewardship Council
FSC

To Amanda, the love of my life. The boys,
Hunter and Austin, and to my Mom and Dad.

ACKNOWLEDGEMENTS

This is a diary of just a year of my life starting at promotion from the Championship to the dreamland of the Premiership with a bit of insight into the past. It has been a long journey from the west coast of the United States to the grounds of the Madejski Stadium. There are so many people that have touched my life and the lives of my family along the way. I have so many to thank for getting me to where I am today - living the dream of playing in the Premier League. Here is a start . . .

Firstly, I'd like to thank my Mom and Dad, Art and Helga, for guiding me and pushing me when I needed it. My wife, Amanda, the best thing that has ever happened to me. My crazy boys, Hunter and Austin, who guarantee that nothing is ever boring. My sister, Diana, who is still so supportive. My father-in-law, Jon, for your patience and joining me on fishing trips. My mother-in-law, Loanna, for your ear and encouraging words.

The people that have coached, counselled, guided and kept me focused on the big picture. Cliff McCrath, Alan Hinton, Paul Barron, John Richardson, Glen "Mooch" Myernick (R.I.P.), Bernie James, Chance Fry, Dicky McCormick, Peter Hattrup, Alan Pardew and Nicky Hammond.

All of my team-mates from the past. Not just including Seattle Pacific University, Seattle Sounders, Colorado Rapids, Fulham and the US National team. I wanted to name you all, but Pat won't let me.

The Goalkeeping Union, the guys I have played with in England: Maik Taylor, Edwin van der Sar, Jamie Ashdown, Jamie Young, Adam Federici and Graham Stack.

The companies that have helped me and believed in me: Jay at Redbird Golf, Ben at Red Bull and Brad and Rob at Nike. To those companies that have been distractors from the pressures of life between the sticks and have happily kept money from burning a hole in my pockets: Northway Porsche, Costco, Lindsey Racing, Wade's Gun Shop, Evening Hatch and the bike stores that helped keep me fit.

The people that have taken my mind off of football when it was much needed: Erik Schippers, who is basically my brother and life-long friend, Ray Northway and Kasey Keller, and Justin Chancellor and the rest of the crew from Tool. The entire RFC staff, especially the coaches, the Gaffer, Kevin Dillon, Wally Downes, Brian McDermott and the guy I work the most closely with, Sal Bibbo, my current GK coach who took me to the promised land. The medical staff, led by Jon Fearn, Andy Stanbury and Goody. They have worked tirelessly and somehow kept me fit for just about every game. Also, the ever-reliable Ron Grant and Selby Armstrong and last, but not least, the unsung heroes of the club, all of the non-playing staff. Without all of you, the machine that we call RFC would not work at all.

Not forgetting Pat Symes, who has spent a lot of time at my house doing interviews while I was making repairs on cars and dodging construction workers and who helped me to down lots and lots of coffee while writing this book. Thanks for putting up with us and for all of the time you gave in what must have been a challenging year for you.

And, of course, to the fans who welcomed me from day one of my arrival at Reading and have stuck by me ever since.

To all I have listed here and to so many more, thank you.

Marcus Hahnemann
August 2007

CONTENTS

PHOTOGRAPHIC ACKNOWLEDGEMENTS

Know The Score Books would like to thank the
following for the use of images in this book: Action
Images, Reading Evening Post, Mike Walker,
Amanda Hahnemann and Mike Green of Mike Green
Photography - www.mikegreenphotography.com

MARCUS HAHNEMANN'S PREMIERSHIP DIARY

FOREWORD

By Graeme Murty, Reading FC captain

The first time I clapped eyes on Marcus it was like The Good, The Bad and The Ugly had taken residence in Berkshire. There he was, this huge 6 foot 3 inch, big, brash, redneck cowboy staring back at me, looking like he should be chewing tobacco and holding a revolver like a true American gunslinger.

At training, our manager at the time, Alan Pardew, asked him to work on a kicking drill and I stood an absolute mile away from him and told Marcus to pick the Boss out with a goal kick. Marcus, who has one of the most distinctive kicking actions in the Premier League, then sent this ball flying a good 35 yards over his head with a rather bemused look on the gaffer's face. "I can cut a bit off it if you like," Marcus said, and that was it, the cult of Hahnemann had truly arrived at Reading Football Club.

You cannot help but like the guy. He is one of the few people whose physical stature and size match his larger-than-life personality. This is coming from someone who used to room with him, until his love of Tool and Slipknot ruined that, but we have developed a strong friendship during the six years we have been together at the club. Whether it be on the golf course or racing around in that lovely white Ford Capri he likes to refer to as a

Porsche, he is one person in football I can truly refer to as a genuine friend.

He is also probably the only footballer in England who, when interviewed about a game, doesn't talk about football. All Marcus likes discussing is music, cars and guns. He will turn up to training wearing a Tool t-shirt, which is fair enough because you think, 'Yes, you are a tool, but what is that all about?' Marcus then goes on to explain everything about his favourite band and has tried countless times to get all the squad to go to one of their concerts. But can you imagine Leroy Lita and Ibrahima Sonko at a Tool gig?

At Reading we always try to be a team and a club that goes the extra mile and Marcus undoubtedly embodies that. He is a true gentleman and a credit to the club and, most importantly, to his family and himself.

I mentioned before about how we originally started out as room-mates before our amicable split. I would often be the one lumbered with listening to his whining. For Marcus nothing in this country seems good enough a lot of the time. English food portions are not big enough, English beds are not big enough and heaven forbid getting him on to the subject of music played in most nightclubs.

The lads' stock response is usually: 'If you don't like it, then bugger off back to America.' But we all know he is only winding us up because he just loves a moan.

Rooming with him therefore was always an interesting experience, especially when he would fall asleep with his iPod on at full volume. Quite often the big man would roll over and out would drop one headphone and therefore I would have to contend with falling asleep the night before a game to the relaxing tones of Slipknot.

Eventually Marcus' hatred of small beds got so much he coaxed Kevin Dillon into allowing him to have his own room on away days. I ended up trading him for James Harper, which is a whole new story in itself really.

Aside from his music and the small arsenal of guns he seems intent on collecting, Marcus' love of life literally in the fast lane is well documented and I have on one occasion had the pleasure of being his front-seat passenger. The Porsche is his pride and joy and Marcus called me up to take it out for a spin. He would often suggest this at the training ground, but the problem with his beloved Porsche was that it would usually only ever work one day a week at best. Anyway, I was strapped in and ready to go, but nothing could prepare me for the sheer gravity-defying adrenaline kick as he pushed his foot to the floor and off we sped down the narrowest, windiest country roads. Marcus had a sadistic grin on as he insisted on showing me how well the car could handle every single corner, again and again and again. Five minutes more and my beef stroganoff would have ended up all over the dashboard.

Mind you, I am keen to get him on the racetrack and see what he can do because I'm sure I could give him a run for his money when there is some competition on the table.

He has also developed a close bond with the Madejski Stadium faithful over the years and it is simply because he is an incredibly likeable, down-to-earth guy who, in a way, idolises the fans as much as they idolise him. His trademark has now become the moment when he throws his jersey into the crowd at the end of the game. When he first did it, a club official gave him a slap on the wrist and told him he had to stop it because it was costing the club too much money. For Marcus that was a small price to pay for rewarding the fans for their loyalty and he knows the simple act of throwing his shirt into the crowd can make someone's day. It is not because he is a poseur or because he likes to lap up the adulation. It is simply because he gets caught up in the moment after a game and sees that as a small way of bridging that gap between players and fans. This is something which the modern game of football seems to be reluctant to address as it gets more corporate and money-orientated.

Despite Americans not always being renowned for their banter, Marcus is one who can take it well and, let's be honest, quite often brings it upon himself. The night we won the Championship title will always be remembered fondly as we all hit the bright lights of Windsor in our club tracksuits to celebrate an historic achievement, but, crucially, without one of the main components of our record-breaking squad. Some way down on the coach from Leicester to Reading Marcus got a call from his lovely wife Amanda asking him to come home rather than spending the evening with the boys. In a shambolic display of cowardice for somebody of his size, the man bowed to Amanda's wishes and left us to join his family. You could see his brain ticking over as she demanded he come home and, despite everybody's disappointment at his no-show, we were not prepared to come between a man and his wife - especially a man who owns about 18 guns. In this book I'm told he has his own version of that story.

For a man who stands that tall, it really is impressive that a person as small as Amanda can tell him what to do all the time. If you need any evidence to back this up you only need to gauge Hunter and Austin's reaction when their dad tells them to do something; they generally ignore him. But when Amanda speaks, the boys listen. Not to say Marcus is a bad dad, he's terrific, but it is fairly obvious who rules the roost in the Hahnemann household.

As a goalkeeper I think our goalkeeping coach at Reading, Sal Bibbo, perhaps best sums it up when he says, "There are not many in the Premier League who could replace Marcus." As an athlete and as a bloke he stands alone and he is top drawer in every department. You do not go through a Championship season losing only two games without being a great goalkeeper. As a defender it is a calming presence to have him standing behind you and it is testament to his ability that he was second only to David James, who had an unbelievable season, in last year's Premiership goalkeeping statistics.

I believe Marcus still has plenty in him to go on for several more seasons, providing he maintains the same focus and intensity he shows every day in training, and I am sure he will. Marcus always wants to be the best and absolutely hates it when he is not. Nothing delights me and the lads more than to wind him up in training by firing balls past him and into the net. Quite often he loses his rag and literally kicks his toys out of the pram by booting all the training balls into the car park nearby. No keeper should like conceding - even in training.

The fact that so much can be said about Marcus is a credit to him as a man and how much he is now part of the fabric of Reading Football Club. Steve Coppell often refers to him as 'the perfect club man' and I cannot disagree with that. He is always one of the first to volunteer for charity events and I have never come across a single person who has not been left with a smile after meeting him. This club, and now the Premier League, would be a poorer place without him and I am sure this season will spring up as many stories as last, with Marcus ready to give his own unique account of everything.

But as for those Tool tickets, he can forget about it.

(As told to James Piercy)

MARCUS HAHNEMANN'S PREMIERSHIP DIARY

APRIL

06

We're going up.

April 1

We are the champions. Today we have beaten Derby 5-0 and nine months of brilliant football, anticipation and pressure is over. Amanda and my boys, Hunter and Austin, are in a crowd approaching 23,000 with Amanda's aunt and two cousins and they are out there joining in the celebrations and soaking up the party atmosphere. The Madejski Stadium is alive with joy and yet I sit in the dressing room almost in disbelief. This is the end of an incredible journey for all of us, but even now I find it hard to describe exactly how I feel.

I have played in every league game and to have played such a significant part makes our success all the more meaningful for me. For a moment or two I have to let it all sink in. My initial reaction is the sort of happiness the fans were enjoying out there, but then comes relief. I say relief because had we failed to win the Championship, it would have been just about the biggest choke in football history. Not to have won it after the way we had played and the results we had put together would have been disastrous. We have been on a knife-edge the whole year and the pressure has been far greater than some people realised. We had been in the top two since August 20th and leaders since November 26th and that creates it own pressure. Everyone was saying to us, "You are going to do it," but we, the players, did not dare believe them, concentrating on winning only the next game. Suddenly it has hit me. We really are the Champions. I phone Amanda, tell her to meet me, grab myself a Red Bull and go back up to sample the incredible atmosphere as fans spill on to the pitch. A lot of hard work has gone into this wonderful conclusion. It is time to enjoy.

April 2

I had been promoted once before to the Premiership when I was number two goalkeeper to Maik Taylor, but this was different, and better. My job at Fulham as back-up keeper was crucial, helping Taylor prepare through the week and on match days. If the strikers wanted extra shooting practice, I stayed behind and let them shoot at me. That was my task, worrying about the other guys, and I took great pride in that. But here at Reading I am number one and the pride is even greater.

At Fulham.

April 3

I think we might have missed a trick at the Derby match. Where were the Championship t-shirts? The club would have made a fortune if they had been available to the crowd after the game, but there was nothing for them to take home as souvenirs or mementoes for the players. There were 'promoted' t-shirts in the club shop, but nothing to say we were champions.When we went up to receive the crowd's applause with our families we were wearing someone else's sweatshirts. This was one of the biggest days in all our lives, players and fans, and I reckon the club could have sold 25,000 of them that day. And it is not as though the club were caught unawares by our success. Another grumble: The club gave us three bottles of champagne and we quickly ran out.

April 4

Many of our fans thought we had won it by Christmas, but none of the players did. The previous year we had slipped up within sight of the finishing post when Dave Kitson was injured. Our defence fell away, caught on counter-attacks, and we all knew how fragile our situation was and how easily it could all go wrong again. I think we knew we were not going to fail this time when we drew 1-1 at Sheffield United on February 14th. I had oe of my best games at Bramall Lane and made one great diving save, which goes down as one of my favourites of the season.

APRIL 06

My save at Sheffield United.

April 5

Football produces so many highs and lows, but it is hard to imagine a greater range of emotions than at Leicester on March 25th. It was here we were promoted, but you would never have known it from our reaction at the final whistle. I, for one, was utterly disappointed. We'd needed to win and had drawn 1-1. As usual I threw my shirt among those crazy Royals fans, but at that stage I felt I had let them down. I was walking back to the dressing room dejected. Then suddenly there was Graeme Murty running back out on to the pitch, his arms aloft. "We are up," yelled Murts. Leeds had drawn and their failure was enough to get us into the Premiership. In five seconds we went from misery to elation, an amazing swing in feelings. Suddenly all hell broke loose. The fans got wind of our promotion and raised the roof, the dressing room went beserk and the champagne flowed. Everything we had striven for had finally come true. As the team bus made its way south, the beer flowed. I guess we must have run out of champagne (again), but then, I hate champagne.

Later that day......

Amanda and the boys had been at Leicester that day and they were as excited and ecstatic as I was. They beat the bus back to the Madejski Stadium where all the cars had been moved for some reason. I drove home expecting to link with the lads later that evening. Murts had suggested a nightclub in Windsor. But when I got back to our home in Pangbourne, half the town had turned out to greet us. There must have been 25 neighbours, friends and well-wishers wandering around our house, drink in hand. It was wonderful, but before long I had had way too much to drink and there was no way I could drive to Windsor. The party was in full swing at home instead. Do you know, I still get stick for not going to that nightclub. Murts has a wicked sense of humour and went on radio and said I had snubbed my team-mates because Amanda would not let me out. The following weekend, I asked the lads who was going out and no-one took me up.

Those crazy Royals.

MARCUS HAHNEMANN'S PREMIERSHIP DIARY

With Hunter and Austin and the Championship trophy.

April 13

The boys are keen Royals fans, but Austin, who is six, sometimes says he wants me to go back to Fulham. He's just being difficult.

April 29

We are building up to our last match of the season at home to Queen's Park Rangers. We need three goals for our hundred and the only players not to have scored so far are Murts and myself. Murts is our longest-serving player, having joined us in 1998, and I know he's desperate to get a goal. So here he is, practicing penalties as if his life depends on it. Murts is a good pal, we are much the same age and play golf together, and his wife Karen and Amanda are close. It would be remarkable if he rounded off the season with a goal of any sort, a long shot from right-back or a penalty. It's not even certain if Murts is going to take a spot-kick if we get one, but it would take a hard man to deny him. Not even Steve Coppell would do that in our position. The bookies even think I might take a penalty and I'm listed at odds of 4-1. My advice is to keep your money in your pocket.

April 30

This is the day we have been waiting for. The Championship trophy is being presented and we also get our medals. The whole of our stadium is awash with blue and white and all we want to do is get the game over and get celebrating. The noise is unbelievable. This is the greatest day in the club's history, after all. QPR don't threaten us, but we are not at our best. And then it happens. We get a penalty and up steps Murts. The last day, the last goal and it's all down to him. As he prepares to take it, I find myself shaking with nerves on his behalf. He's never going to believe that. The place goes silent. Murts smashes the ball into the net past the substitute keeper Jake Cole and races off on an extravagant celebration, ending only when he collides on the touchline with Kingsley, our well-padded lion mascot. The place erupts and Murts is swamped by his teammates. We win the game, of course, as we had done 30 other league matches. All that remains is for us to collect our medals and the trophy and then comes the fantastic lap of honour around the pitch. Those scenes of jubilation will live with me forever.

Sonko, Me, Murts, Shorey and Ingi enjoy the celebrations after the QPR game.

MAY

06

Open-top celebrations.

May 1

Today we are to take an open-topped bus ride through the streets of Reading to receive the cheers and the acclaim of the town. This has been planned since March, which I thought was the dumbest thing ever since it was way too soon. The players, coaching staff and others were to be on one bus and the families on another. I'm not sure this is the best way, but you are never going to keep everyone happy.

From the stadium we go to the bus depot and I have this horrible feeling that this is all going to be very embarrassing. At the depot there must have been all of three fans waiting for us and I fear it's going to be the same all around town. There are other things to do on a Bank Holiday Monday. But as the buses reach the station, a sight awaits us which even now makes me emotional just to talk about it. The streets are lined with our fans, ten deep, hanging from lights, shop signs, anything. The noise is deafening and goes on and on and on. We are all just blown away by the sheer size of the reception. Even the side streets are full of jubilant Royals fans, a never-ending sea of blue and white. There are estimates of 100,000 people, but who knows?

Eventually we get back to the stadium and the place is packed. My parents, Artur and Helga, are over from Seattle and I don't think they have ever seen anything like this. On the pitch, my boys 'tackle' Murts, I go in goal and try to save a few penalties. A girl from the crowd comes on and scores a penalty against me. It is that sort of day.

The crowds line the streets.

MARCUS HAHNEMANN'S PREMIERSHIP DIARY

Later that day.....

There is a celebratory Ball at the stadium. I barely have time to go home and get changed. My parents enjoyed the dancing, but by now all I want to do is go home and go to bed.

May 3

Sheffield United are going up with us. Watford may follow if they can beat Leeds in the play-off final. That would mean three small clubs in the Premiership next season and all any of us will want to do is survive. There is a sort of camaraderie among the little clubs. We all rooted for Wigan when they went up and they have shown us that it is possible to prosper once you get there. Well done, Wigan. As for Watford, our friend Dave, the manager at Costco where we do some of our shopping, is a big fan of theirs. He has had to listen to me telling him how well Reading have done, as if he did not know.

May 5

Bruce Arena, the coach of the United States national team, has announced his squad for the World Cup and I'm in it, which is fantastic news. Kasey Keller, an old friend and now playing in Germany for Borussia Moenchengladbach, is going to be number one goalkeeper I feel sure, but it's between me and Tim Howard as to who is going to be his deputy. Tim is at Manchester United, but didn't get a Premiership start for them in the season just finished. At least I played every league game bar one for Reading.

May 6

All the other Reading players can look forward to six weeks of resting and relaxing, but not me. The USA want me over in North Carolina for a training camp. At 33, this is my first World Cup and coming so soon after Reading's promotion, this is a wonderful time. The problem with being a goalkeeper is that only one can play, so if Kasey is chosen ahead of me I have to face the fact that I won't get a game. But just being there in Germany, the birthplace of my parents and in Hamburg, where the USA are scheduled to play and be based and where mom and dad actually come from, is unbelievable. I would love to play, of course, but I am not going to lose any sleep if I don't.

May 11

Training is going well and morale in the American camp is high. I get along with Bruce well. Plenty of free time with my golf clubs in tow. So there's always time for a round, but the only difference is Murts is not here for me to beat. His camps are always enjoyable and he's a good golfer and I love golf too. Most of all I like beating Murts. I see my selection for the national squad as reward for my club form and it's good to catch up with the other guys. At my age, I'm just grateful to be there.

May 14

One of the things I like about Bruce is that he runs a very relaxed camp. He does not insist we all eat together all of the time. We have breakfast on our own or in groups, lunch as a squad, but then for the evening meal he lets us do what we want. You hear some horror stories about other countries where the management insist everyone is locked together all of the time, I guess to prevent cliques forming. I would hate that. People can get sick of each other. Not everybody is the same. For instance at Reading, Bobby Convey and I have the fact that we are the only Americans in the squad as a reason to keep an eye out for each other. We get on well. But in a squad full of Americans, you gravitate to those of a similar age and interests. Kasey Keller and Landon Donovan share my love for the heavy metal band Tool and we are older than some of the others. Bobby hangs out with Eddie Pope and the younger guys. Some other countries tie their players to all kinds of regulations and schedules, but Bruce reckons we can look after ourselves.

May 15

I may not be first choice, but that is no reason not to give 100 per cent and more on the training ground. I'm happy to stay behind after training to help the forwards with shooting practice, if that's what they want, as I did when I was number two at Fulham. The banter is good and it's enjoyable playing with people you know. There is great excitement because this is as good as it gets for most of us and it's a chance to show the world that football is alive and well in America. We have three tough group matches, but there is a feeling that we can get beyond that.

Getting in the mood.

May 17

All the USA's World Cup build-up games have been poor and I don't get to play in any of them. We beat Latvia, Angola and Venezuela, but lose to Morocco. I have a feeling that I may end up behind Tim in the pecking order, but it's going to be a great adventure. There are absolutely no complaints from me and the experience is going to be all the greater for having Amanda, the boys, my parents, Amanda's parents, my sister and her family and all my German relatives there in Hamburg. It would be nice if they could actually see me play, but at this stage all I can do is train hard and prepare properly. Any day now and we are off to Germany.

JUNE

06

American fans join the World Cup party.

June 5

Hamburg. Already my knowledge of the German language is proving pretty handy. At home when I was growing up in Seattle we spoke it some of the time, almost as much as English, because of my parents' heritage, but it can get rusty. I must have been to Hamburg five or six times before, visiting relations, so I know what to expect. It's a clean, modern city and a nice place for the US team to be based.

June 6

The day started off like most others here in Germany. We trained in the morning and were just hanging out in the hotel. When I saw Pam Perkins, the US team organiser, in the hallway she asked me if I would be interested in going to a rock concert that night. "Who is it?" was my response. She looked through her paperwork and wondered out loud why we were able to go tonight, but not the night before when the Eagles (a band she really likes) were performing. "Tool," she said finally. I said "I'm in" and so was Kasey. I told her Landon, Brian Ching and Jimmy Conrad would probably also want to go.

June 9

The World Cup is under way, Germany against Costa Rica. Bruce has told me that Kasey will be number one, as I expected, but Tim will be his first deputy. I have to say from a selfish point of view I'm a little disappointed, but I'm only a red card or a thigh strain away from playing. It's a long time since I was a back-up keeper, but it all comes back to me, all the hard work during the week and then not playing, when Bruce gives me the bad news. It sucks, but what can I do? Just being here is tremendous.

June 10

Germany have won 4-2 the previous day and World Cup fever is beginning to build in Hamburg, the city my parents left in the mid-'60s when my father joined Boeing in Seattle. Dad had always loved his football, but played no sport when he was growing up because he had to work (so he says) and reckons he missed out. That is why he always insisted my older sister Diana and I played as much sport as possible and why, indirectly I guess, I am here taking a minor part in football's biggest tournament.

June 11

Amanda, Hunter and Austin fly out today and will stay for the duration of the World Cup, at least for the group stage and hopefully longer. I am going to have plenty of support. I reckon about 25 are coming over from the United States and there are relatives all over the place here in Hamburg. It would be nice if they all got to see me play, but that would mean something happening to Kasey and Tim and I genuinely don't want that. My parents are over, of course, as is my sister. This is a great chance to see the World Cup, possibly me in action and catch up with all the relations and friends they left behind.

Dad and Mom have arranged a house swap with one of our relatives. They are going to explore America from my parents' house in Seattle and we will be able to use their home in Hamburg as a refuge from the hotel. Our management have been far-sighted in allowing the families to stay in the same hotel as the team. They are staying on a different floor and it's

Our whole crew, hoping that I get onto the pitch
from the bench, at the World Cup.

not as though they are going to distract us from what we have to do. We are here to play in the World Cup and that's all that matters, but it is comforting to know I can see them every day. My family are the most important people in my life. Dad, Mom, Diana and her family and my in-laws are in a hotel just down

JUNE 06

the road. Anne-Marie van der Sar, wife of Edwin, the Dutch goalkeeper, and a friend of ours, could not believe wives and families were allowed in the same hotel as the team. We have also arranged transportation for wives, girlfriends and relatives for every match in a chartered 747.

June 12

This is it, our first game. The Czech Republic turn us over 3-0 and we don't play well. There's a crowd of 52,000 in the Veltins Arena, Gelsenkirchen, including Arsène Wenger to look at his new boy Tomas Rosicky and he must be glad he got him. Claudio Reyna hits the inside of a post for us at 1-0 and that could have changed the course of our whole World Cup, but there are no complaints from any of us. There is just a moment when it suddenly occurs to me that Rosicky, who scores two great goals for the Czechs, will be a Premiership opponent for me next season. On the bench, there is time to think about such things.

June 14

My biggest problem is my weight. I love food and the spread before us at meal-times here at our hotel is ridiculous. Every meal is an adventure and I look forward to them with excitement. There are usually three or four main dishes and I grab everything because they all look so good. There are

Amanda's dad, Jon Day, outside a Hamburg Beer Keller.

chocolate cakes, six different types of ice cream and for two weeks I sample just about the best food I have ever eaten. It's not just meals. There is a lounge in the hotel where permanently on display is a full range of all the foods I used to love in the United States, but can't get in England. Things like peanut butter jelly. I have to eat them. This is wonderful. It's a good thing that the gym is in the hotel.

A rare family moment at the USA team hotel in Hamburg during the World Cup.

JUNE 06

June 15

Today is my 34th birthday. I celebrate with a typically delicious German cake filled with cream. I get to see Amanda and the boys for about two minutes because we are putting the finishing touches to our preparations. The other players somehow find out it's my birthday and enjoy pointing out my age.

June 17

We travel to Kaiserslautern to the Fritz Walter Stadion. Opponents Italy are one of the favourites and any kind of positive result is going to be great for us. And we get it in a 1-1 draw. Brian McBride's face is a mass of blood after being elbowed by Daniele De Rossi who gets sent off. But we end up with nine men. Pablo Mastroeni is also sent off and Eddie Pope then follows for two yellow cards. Not much goes right except for the result, which was our reward for digging in and fighting. I find the refs are poor and not much goes for us. I also find it much more difficult being on the bench when all the decisions are going against us. I find myself yelling more like a fan than a goalkeeper, encouraging my team more than ranting at the officials. I think the refs get the brunt of it. When you are on the field you have to concentrate right away and get on with it and start organising your defence and yourself.

Brian McBride's bleeding nose after the elbow
from Italy's Daniele De Rossi.

June 20

Now the food spreads we have at the hotel are a joke. There is an unbelievable amount available. Well, we are Americans, so I shouldn't need to say any more. But for sheer choice, it was hard to pick. I usually ended up with a sampler plate, but I think it resembled a food mountain. Murts would have said, "Do you want a flag in that?" So to have any chance of playing next English season that means a daily trip to the gym for a date with the Concept 2 rowing machine.

June 21

The thing that amazes me every day was the security. We had our own US-based secret service agents and it looked like the whole Hamburg SWAT team protecting us daily. With the current world situation, no-one was taking any chances. I have a huge interest in guns and I collect them in the States. When I'm back in Seattle I try to make as many detours as possible to Wade's indoor range and gun shop. At the 25 yard range I shoot anything from my AR-15 to a variety of hand guns. It is as addictive trying to get a bullseye as trying to perfect my performance on the football pitch. So it's always interesting to see what our security force is packing.

June 22

Five days after the Italy match, we are in Nuremburg to face Ghana. As if the Italian game was not exhausting enough, we need to win this or we all go home. Kasey is in goal again for the third time, so I resign myself to not getting a game, but just being here is still awesome. The first two group matches didn't go our way and it's the same here. Reyna was fouled and for the first time in the World Cup they don't blow the whistle. No penalty. This lets in Ghana for the

With my sister, Diana Bowar, at the World Cup.

lead, but Clint Dempsey equalises just before half-time. There is hope. But that disappears in no time when Ghana get a soft penalty and score the winner from it. End of story, end of our World Cup. I don't know why, but so few marginal decisions ever seemed to go our way. To lose by a controversial penalty is hard enough to take at the best of times, but this is the biggest tournament in football. I'm told Manchester United get a lot of penalties at home. I shall find out next season, but then they do attack a lot.

June 23

We get ready to go home and I can start thinking about a holiday. My Reading pals will be back in training in three weeks. They will probably have been watching the World Cup in beach bars around the world, but they would have waited a long time if they wanted a glimpse of me. The inquest begins. This is Bruce Arena's last big tournament and I guess the same for many of our players. Bruce says we didn't attack enough. "It was not our time," was his phrase. Games are decided by inches, like when Reyna hit the inside of that post. Over a 38-game Premiership season there is time for luck to even itself out, but here we had three games and the inches were against us. The bottom line is that we didn't get enough goals, so perhaps Bruce was right. It was not our time.

June 24

The American team breaks up and goes home. It's quite possible I won't see some of these guys again as international team-mates. Our team was not the youngest in the tournament, and life has to move on. There will be changes, younger players brought in and groomed for four years down the line. Right now all I want to do

The Hahnemann clan hit the World Cup! (back row from l to r) Myself, mom, Sara Bowar, Nick Bowar, Diana Bowar, Amanda, Art, Dale Bowar (front row) Austin, Hunter, Ashley, Loanna Day.

is head back to Seattle with Amanda and our children and see something of the city and our family and friends. My parents, my sister, her family and my in-laws are back in Seattle now, so we will see plenty of them too. For three weeks football should be forgotten, but even now I am thinking of the Premiership in unguarded moments and I can't help but be excited.

JULY

06

The boys digging clams on the beach at Amanda's parents' house in Seabeck.

July 1

I'm doing as little as possible, that's what holidays are for. First stop is my buddy's to see the Cherokee jeep, which we modified together. It has 35 inch tyres and is really cool. He sent me a video of it in the snow and I just wish I had been there. I love cars. I have seven of them, a few like the Cherokee in Seattle and the rest in England. Tinkering with cars is my greatest relaxation and when I'm back at Reading I spend winter afternoons after training, tuning and improving my Porsche. In fact I think I prefer working on my cars than actually driving them. I have been known to fix something that was not really broken.

July 2

The kids love Seattle. Two sets of grandparents make a fuss of them and they get to sample what Amanda and I grew up with. There are mountains, a fresh water lake and the Hood canal and wide, open spaces, which we miss. Amanda's parents live on the saltwater canal, where I keep my boat. It's more of a fishing boat, but you can ski or wake board behind it. This is my chance to use it. Seattle's closeness to the mountains means it's perfectly possible to ski and water ski on the same day. I haven't done it, but I know people who have. I love skiing, but Steve Coppell would shudder if he thought I was still doing it. I guess I will have to wait until I have retired from football before I take it up again.

Amanda writes........

My dad Jon Day and mom Loanna owned Seabeck Shellfish Farm, about an hour from the city, and I spent an idyllic childhood on, in or near the sea. I sold oysters and clams and didn't realise how much the sea was part of me until I moved away from it. Dad was also a marine biologist and teacher and my mother was an elementary school psychologist and I have an older brother, Nathan, who has been over to see us and watch Marcus play. There is a stream of visitors from America to our home in Pangbourne, so it's not as though we ever lose touch. I miss the sea. Just looking at it has a calming effect and gives a peace of mind.

July 5

After yesterday's huge Independence Day celebrations, Amanda and I take Hunter and Austin to catch crabs, clams and oysters. They also swim in the fresh water lake near to where my sister lives, so they associate Seattle with summer holidays. But the climate over here is similar to England and there are real winters as well. It's strange.

The American people really got into the World Cup and the interest surprised me. My mom made sure I was the centre of attention by telling everyone she met I was in it. A year or two ago I could have gone back to Seattle in total anonymity, but this time, once or twice I get recognised.

We spent yesterday with the whole family at Amanda's parent's house by the side of the water at Seabeck for the 4th of July celebrations. All the boys were shooting off their own fireworks that they had bought at a Native American) reservation.

Relaxing with my dog Mazzy back in the US.

July 6

If it had not been for my dad's insistence that I played any kind of sport, I might never have played football professionally and Reading would be just a rock festival to me. It all comes back to my car fetish. When I was 15, dad bought me a car, a 412 Volkswagen, which we worked on together, but then I sold it and made a small profit. In its place I bought a Volkswagen Thing, a rare military-style jeep, and, with manual in hand, I taught myself what happened under a bonnet. Dad was always on hand if there was something I didn't understand. All my buddies were into cars and we worked on each other's. Amanda and I courted in that car and we have it still today, that and the 94 Cherokee. Anyway, at 16 I had reached the age where I preferred cars to sport and wanted to give up playing. I had done basketball, baseball, soccer, American football. You name it. Yes, I was good at sport, but there was no obvious future in it and I just loved my car. Dad gave me an ultimatum when he bought me my first Volkswagen: You can have the car, but you must carry on playing sport, any sport of your choice. "Okay," I said, "I enjoy football the best and goalkeeping best of all. It's a deal."

Tinkering with the engine of my Porsche
at Northway Porsche: I love spending time with my cars.

July 12

The Reading players will be reporting for training soon, but I'm still unwinding, still doing the rounds of friends and relatives. Many of those we were at school and university with are still here. Like us, they are over 30 and in some cases with youngsters of their own. They are intrigued a little by me, a professional soccer player living abroad, and by our English lifestyle. Amanda and I wonder what we would have been like had we stayed in Seattle. In a way it's still home. We have a house here and our family are all around, but we have been away a long time and there are roots in the Berkshire countryside.

July 14

Paul Barron, the Middlesbrough goalkeeper coach, and a former Arsenal and West Bromwich Albion player, was a big influence in my early development. Every summer, the English close season, he came over to coach at Seattle Pacific University, where Amanda and I went to school, and could see my improvement. I was making a big reputation in college football with a high number of shut-outs in a successful team. I fancied playing abroad, in fact it was a dream. But he couldn't see a way I could get into England until I pointed out that I had a German passport and could get a work permit, no problem. But it was Alan Hinton who got me my first trial in England at Sheffield Wednesday in the mid-90s. Alan got three England caps and came out to join Seattle Sounders at the end of his career, then stayed on after the collapse of the old NASL. He bought the Sounders name. David Pleat was the Wednesday manager and his main keepers were Chris Woods and Kevin Pressman. I found the training was fantastic, the facilities incredible and the whole atmosphere superb. I could only improve. I knew then that I wanted more of this. This was what I wanted to do. But I went home again without getting a game of any kind.

July 15

Today I think back and as a kid I might have joined Stuttgart or Aston Villa or even West Ham. I trained with them all in the off-seasons. I was playing for Seattle and then Colorado Rapids in the Major League Soccer, but coming to Europe when it was possible. In 1995 Amanda and I were on honeymoon. We actually spent our honeymoon not in Mexico as we had planned, but in Florence after I had been selected to play for a World XI as back up to the Brazilian Tafarrel. On the way back we spent a couple of weeks in England while I trained with West Ham. Harry Redknapp was the manager and I think I impressed him. He wanted me to stay longer. But I told him I had a plane to catch next day and he didn't try to stop me. I went to Aston Villa another year when Paul Barron fixed me a trial. They had Spink, Oakes and Bosnich as goalkeepers and I don't think I was ready for England. Bosnich was a surprise. Unlike most of us, he did all his warm-ups inside before going out to the training pitch.

July 16

The fixtures are out for our first Premiership season and by a strange coincidence we are at home to Paul Barron's Middlesbrough on the first day. I can't emphasise enough how big a part he played in getting me involved seriously in soccer. When he came over to Seattle he used to tell me I was too fat and hammered me for my laid-back attitude, but he could see my potential. In those days I didn't much care. I was having fun. When I was playing professionally for Seattle in the A League, I trained in the morning and did nothing in the afternoon. Bernie James, another of my mentors and a Seattle teammate, painted houses for a living. I helped him one day and that was enough. I felt like I was cheating life, playing soccer for a living.

Amanda making brownies, as she does for the whole team for every away match.

July 18

On holiday I have to watch my weight. I don't want anyone calling me fat again. At Reading they think I carry too much sometimes. Sal Bibbo, our goalkeeping coach, Darren Roberts, our nutritionist and Jon Goodman, the sports scientist, all gather round when it's my turn to be weighed, and mutter. Amanda makes sure I stay away from pasta and other fattening foods and I have to be disciplined, but it's hard. I weigh 106 kilos at best.

MARCUS HAHNEMANN'S PREMIERSHIP DIARY

July 19

To go back to Paul, it must have been about 1998 when he told me he thought I could make it in England and that he thought Villa wanted me. But back then Amanda was pregnant with Hunter and by now I was playing under contract for Colorado and we were settled where we were. The ambition was still to play in Europe, but not right then. Villa signed Peter Enckelman instead early in '99. I had another year of my contract at Colorado to go, but I decided to get an agent and send videos to British clubs. Paul said he was doing more work for Marcus Hahnemann than any agent.

Amanda writes.......

I met Marcus at SPU. I was studying exercise science and we first came across each other in a general education class. I wanted to go into sports management. I got to know him better when I went to watch a Vancouver Canucks hockey match with his hockey-mad room-mate, Alan Chase. We hit it off straight away and have been together pretty much ever since. We are best friends. I played football as a child and carried it on at university. All the kids growing up play football. My brother played, so there was nothing strange about Marcus doing it as a job. Cliff McCrath, one of Marcus's soccer coaches and an ordained minister, married us on December 22, 1995, just about the only time there was a gap in the American soccer calendar. Or so we thought. I had graduated a couple of weeks before the wedding and was looking forward to our Mexican honeymoon at an all-inclusive resort. But then Marcus got a call to play for this World XI against Fiorentina, a great honour, and of course we had to go. We had the best suite in the hotel and while I slept in luxury, Marcus had to go off training.

We lived in a basement flat at the home of Marcus's sister and her husband at first and I became a personal trainer while he played professionally for Seattle.

July 20

I am going to have to return soon to England to catch up with training at Reading. I feel relaxed and ready. It's going to be a huge adventure and I can't help thinking about it. In the space of maybe four months I have achieved two goals in helping Reading to promotion and being involved in a World Cup. Now, all being well, I will fulfil a third by playing in the Premiership.

July 21

Here in Seattle I can see why I was nearly seduced into staying. The scenery is unbelievable, the lakes, the seafood. The Olympic Mountains rise to the west and the Cascade mountain range form a majestic backdrop to the east. From our home, I could be skiing in an hour or water skiing in ten minutes. We are two and a half hours from the Canadian border and California is to the south. I had no desire to go anywhere else. The college team and then playing for Seattle in the A League took me to other campuses and other parts of America and there was nowhere I liked better than home.

July 22

It's going to be hard saying goodbye to all our friends and family, but it has to happen. I realise a little of what it must have been like for my parents to quit Germany in their 20s and head into the unknown for a new life, not even speaking the language. But we get to see them a lot. Dad is semi-retired now, but he had a deep love of football and did some coaching in Seattle. His team was SV Hamburg, but he was brought up by his aunt and dad said he had to deliver bread at 5am every day. There was no time for sport in his early life and that's why he was insistent my sister and I played as much sport as we could, and why indirectly I'm at

Kayaking on Seabeck Bay near Amanda's parents' house.

Reading now. I guess I owe him a lot with that ultimatum of his. No sport, no car. In fairness, once I had chosen to play football, he paid the tax, insurance and for the fuel. I think he knew I was no academic. Mathematics was my best subject and when I first went to SPU I was studying electrical engineering. But I got bored with it and switched to a four-year physical education degree to include anatomy, physiology and bio-mechanics.

July 23

I should say a little more about Bernie James. After I finished a very successful college career at 22, I got a 30,000 dollars a year contract with Seattle Sounders after an open trial. Here I got a lucky break. Dusty Hudock, the keeper at the University of Washington, and I went to the same trial. We both played and both signed for the Sounders. But when I got into the team, we won and when he played we lost. On that basis alone, I became number one and my career took off. Anyway, Bernie James was, and still is, one of the best players I have ever come across. No-one in England would have heard of him because he never played here. Even in America he wasn't a star because soccer is not so prominent. But he was a great talent and deserved a bigger stage. We had a super team. There was Dicky McCormick, Gary Heal, Chance Fry, Peter Hattrup and Gary Megson's brother, Neil. We won the A League championship and played in front of crowds of 3,000. In the final it was 10,000. But today I think back to Bernie. He was a centre-back and a player of unbelievable ability. If he had got to Europe, and I think his mother was English, he could have been a sensation.

The boys enjoying the fork lift with Uncle Pat at his boat shop.

July 24

Today I am heading back to England to get ready for the Premiership. I'm really excited about it all. The good news is that I have missed all the hard work, the running in the heat and all the basics, which every player has to do to get fit. I'm still on a Championship contract, so I would like to think Reading will reward me and the others for what we achieved. I was one of five Reading players named in the Championship team of the season, but you can take nothing for granted. There is always an element of insecurity. Until we kick off against Middlesbrough I still can't call myself a Premiership player.

I remember how I discovered that Fulham, where I was number two to Maik Taylor, had signed Edwin van der Sar. We had just gone up to the Premiership and I'd hoped to be on the bench again, or better. I was watching Fox TV in America when I heard about Edwin and realised I was now number three. Here at Reading we have Graham Stack and Adam Federici, both good keepers, and who is to say Steve Coppell won't bring in another?

July 27

I will talk more of Steve Coppell later, but it's only right I give him credit here for what he did in getting this strange group of individuals into the Premiership. For those of us who were used to Alan Pardew, it took us a year to come to terms with Steve. Alan is volatile, Steve is not. Steve led us to the Holy Grail and while he didn't do it solely by himself, the Coppell imprint was on the team. Promotion was the end of two years' hard work. We never did anything different in matches or on the training ground. Steve does not say a whole lot, but when something needs to be said, he will say it. He once said to us, "There is no telling what you can accomplish if none of you cares who gets the credit." He is right. But in front of him are a group of Americans, Ecuadorians, Senegalese, Icelanders, Cameroonians, Irish and, yes, some English. The team spirit is brilliant considering how everyone is so different. We all come together to play for Reading and for Steve Coppell. Never does he criticise us as a team or as individuals in public. Even in the privacy of the training ground, very rarely does he even hint at a player screwing up. Only once did he get angry at a collective performance. "I will always stand by you, but you guys were crap," he said. It was the only time he disassociated himself from us, or needed to.

July 30

There is a strong American connection among Premiership goalkeepers. Tim Howard is going to Everton, Brad Friedel is as commanding as ever at Blackburn and Kasey Keller, now playing in Germany, spent many years here. Why do we produce so many keepers? A couple of reasons, I think. We grew up playing basketball, American football and sports where you need hand-eye co-ordination. And people in the States want to be goalies. It is a more respected position than in a lot of places in the world. In other countries, the worst player goes in goal. But look at ice hockey in America. As soon as the game is over, everyone goes to congratulate the net-minder.

July 31

Maybe if more kids in England played cricket, there might be more top goalkeepers. My boys love cricket. They play it in the back yard with the kids next door. I wasn't too sure what was going on at first, but they grew up with those guys and that's all they want to do in the summer. That and football. We still get the baseball out once in a while and they smack that about too.

AUGUST

06

The Big Kick Off.

Early August

We are stuck in Sweden, beating some really bad opposition, one of them by a huge number of goals. Some of the guys are getting restless because the Premiership is not going to be like this. The gaffer wanted to break us in gently, but there is nothing to be gained from knocking over teams by ten goals except for a bit of confidence. Still, there's Feyenoord coming up as our major pre-season friendly and that will give us a clearer idea of what we need to do.

August 8

Promotion brought us a nice little bonus. We had a week in Spain before the final match against Queen's Park Rangers where we unwound with a few drinks and some golf, and then, of course, there was the cash. Some of the others spent it on expensive wrist watches, I indulged my passion for cars. I have four of them in England. For a long time I had wanted some custom-built shock absorbers for my Porsche 944 S2. I paid £1,200 on the front shocks and £1,000 for the rears and they make the vehicle a lot quicker and safer. I love my cars and most of all I love tinkering with them in the afternoons after training at a garage owned by my buddy and best friend outside football, Ray Northway. For me it's a great way to forget about football for a bit. I belong to a club and we have track days where we can drive our cars at places like Silverstone and Donnington Park. At Silverstone one time, I blew up a gear box overtaking someone, fast. But if I had to choose between track days and modifying my cars, I would take the tinkering around any time. Ray is a lifelong West Ham fan, but we don't talk football too much. I find that really relaxing.

With Ray Northway, owner of Northway Porsche, where I work on my car, holding the Championship trophy.

August 9

I had a Porsche 911 when I was at Fulham, but I had to sell it when we came to Reading. I took a huge pay cut in order to play regular football and this was the price I had to pay. The 911 was used as the down payment for our house in Pangbourne. But it had to be done and we love living where we do. If I had to choose the car of my dreams, in this country it would be a Porsche 911 RS or GT2. I think I prefer the older Porsches.

August 10

What's the fastest I have ever driven? 135mph top speed in my car on a driving course, but in Germany, where there is no upper speed limit on certain roads, it was on an autobahn in a Porsche 911 owned by Kasey Keller and we were overtaken by an Audi TT. Kasey said, "You're not going to let him get away with that, are you?" and the challenge was on. When we finally overtook the Audi we had been doing 150. I guess Steve Coppell might not have been too pleased about that.

August 11

Before we move on to football, I had better tell you all about my cars. In England Amanda and I have a Jeep Cherokee diesel, a Grand Voyager, a GMC Typhoon and, of course, my Porsche. In America, there's the Volkswagen Thing from when Amanda and I first got together, a Ford Excursion Turbo diesel, which is the biggest SUV ever made, and a lifted Jeep Cherokee. The Typhoon has been badly neglected. One of the things I most enjoy about England is my cars.

August 12

Today we are playing Feyenoord. It's one of Dirk Kuyt's last matches for them before he joins us in the Premiership at Liverpool. Our stadium is a sell-out and the atmosphere is incredible. There is a terrific enthusiasm about the place as the first day of the season gets closer. I think to myself, 'It's going to be like this every week', and one or two of the other guys are thinking and saying the same. A couple of fans say to me they are worried Steve has not been busier in the transfer market. To this point we have signed two players from lower division clubs, Seol Ki-Hyeon and Sam Sodje and, like the rest of us, have never played in the Premiership. I guess they figured we would be spending heavily on big names, but that's not the Reading way. Steve knows our financial limitations and moves in areas other managers don't touch too often.

August 14

It's Monday and we start training today for our first Premiership match at home to Middlesbrough. I guess it could have been tougher, but a few weeks later we play all the big four in a cluster and that could be the key to our whole season. If we can get a few points early on, we may get some confidence and build on that. But no one is saying anything other than the need to survive. If Wigan can do it, so can we. We are taking it easy and there is the usual dressing room banter. Stephen Hunt is bouncing all over the place and Glen 'Blakey' Little is trying to cut any tension with his jokes and his impersonations.

August 16

Three days to go and Chris Makin goes to Southampton, the first of the Championship winners to move on. Chris was not a regular, but he played enough games to get a medal and with no sign of any new contracts being offered, we wonder if he's the first of many. Football is an insecure game. We don't all earn the same as Wayne Rooney and I'm 34.

August 18

One day to go and there is a feeling of expectancy everywhere you go, the town, the training ground at Hogwood Park. It is hard to get away from it. Even when I'm at Ray's garage, staring at a car engine, the heart skips a beat or two at the thought. Each week a big new opponent. Will the novelty wear off?

The Madejski stadium in pristine condition
for the start of the season.

What a start! Leroy Lita celebrates his winner
against Middlesbrough.

August 19

The big day has arrived. Reading versus Middlesbrough in the Barclays Premiership. I am looking forward to seeing Paul Barron again. How weird that as Middlesbrough's goalkeeping coach, he should be here for my first match after all he has done for me in the past. I'm sure he wants his own club to win, but I like to think he wants me to come out of it with some credit. We said to ourselves that Middlesbrough was a good team to play against, first up. But then you look at their line up and there's guys like Yakubu, Mark Viduka, super, super players by any standards and individually more costly than our whole team put together. This is not going to be easy, just easier than Manchester United or someone.

Later.......

The stadium is alive, as if the fans never went home after the QPR game. Paul Barron wishes me good luck. But before we know it, we are 2-0 down. The left winger Stewart Downing smashes a shot past me with tremendous power and accuracy. Nothing like that happened in the whole of last season. It had 'welcome to the Premier League' written all over it. Then a free kick - I can't remember who took it - hits the turf and takes a big bounce into my chest and Yakubu gets to the rebound first. What have we let ourselves in for?

At the kick off I was undeniably nervous about the unknown. Now I am disappointed with the goals, particularly Yakubu's. Should I have saved it? But as I think about all this, that tremendous self-belief and desire of ours comes surging back and before Middlesbrough know what's hit them, Kitson and Sidwell have scored to send us in level at half-time. Steve Coppell is calm. No rants from him. He could see we were on top and made no mention of the goals we had let in. That's not his way either. We go back out determined to win. We are super solid defensively and Lita gets our winner. I can hardly describe what the dressing room was like afterwards. It was like we had won two games.

Above all, there was relief. We can relax and look forward to a nice day off. It was not something we talked about, but the sooner we got our first win, the less the pressure was going to be. We are here, we said to ourselves. As for Paul Barron, he's not too happy.

Later still.......

Another of the things I like about England is fish and chips. On Saturday evenings, if there is no training next day, I buy fish and chips and Chinese and Indian takeaways. I know it's an unusual combination, but I like them all. I can get the fish and chips and the Indian from the same place no more than 100 yards from home. Often we have as many as 15 people round to join our dinner and tonight I'm really enjoying myself. It's a summer evening and the world is wonderful. I sleep like a baby.

August 20

Sunday. I'm still thinking about those Middlesbrough goals, but I'm not as wound-up as I can be. Sometimes the excitement lingers into the evening after a match and spills into the next day. I try to be positive, but if I'm not, Amanda bears the brunt of my frustration. I have been known to stay up until 4am with my Xbox after a game, replaying match incidents over and over again in my mind. Should I have come for that cross? Should I have left my line? That sort of thing.

August 21

Hunter and Austin enjoyed the Middlesbrough match. All the kids at their school know who I am and they love playing and watching. If they get half as much enjoyment out of football as I have done over the years, then they will have had a great time. They put the serious world of football in perspective. Austin saw me looking sad one Saturday evening. "What's the matter,

Dave Kitson scores our first Premiership goal.
Unfortunately, he is then injured - a big loss for the club.

Dad?"he asked. "I lost my game," I told him. He put his arm around me in consolation. "Don't worry. We'll find it in the morning."

August 22

Dave Kitson was injured against Middlesbrough and it doesn't look good. Kitson was a big player for us last season and we are going to miss him if his knee doesn't improve quickly. We've still got Leroy Lita and Kevin Doyle, who were fantastic last season as well. Doyle just came from nowhere and surprised us all. He looked great in training, but you can't tell much from that. But from the moment he got in the team he started banging in the goals. Unbelievable. He's a great guy, not quiet or loud, down-to-earth and popular with everyone. The only outward sign of his rise to local fame is his 8-series BMW. Otherwise he's still the amiable lad from Ireland. Leroy's super flash with his bling and his yellow Nike's and his giant

Hummer. But he works hard at his game, staying behind after training for extra work. He's got all the tools, fast, good in the air, and this could be a big year for him.

August 23

No sooner had we got Middlesbrough out of our system, then along comes Aston Villa away. Kitson's not fit, but we've got Villa and Wigan in three or four days, the sort of teams we need to get points from. Doyle scores for us and at 1-0 we are in control. Then comes one of those penalty decisions which leave me baffled. Ibrahima Sonko brings down one of their players and gets sent off. It's one of those incidents you see more and more of, where a forward gets in front of a defender and then slows down, almost inviting the tapping of a heal. Sonks tried to get out the way, but he had nowhere else to go but into the back of the forward. It was accidental contact, crazy. Sonks is sent off and banned for the next game, punished twice. I think refs are under orders and I guess it's difficult for them. To be sent off is harsh, but it's super harsh losing him for the next game. Fans pay good money to see the best players and Sky TV the same. As for penalties, you get all kinds of instructions about which way to dive. All the stats said go right when Juan Pablo Angel takes a penalty, this time he goes left. I'm best off making my own decision, to figure it out myself.

August 24

I'm reflecting on a 2-1 defeat instead of a 1-0 win. Take away all the injustices, we have lost and after the year we just had, that's something we are not used to. Now we have to prepare for Wigan without Sonks.

August 25

I think back to the last time I was at Wigan. The pitch was invaded by their jubilant fans, celebrating promotion. They are a little club, like ours, and there is a certain affinity. I never felt threatened when they all poured on. What I remember most is thinking how I wanted the same for our fans. The look of pleasure and happiness on the faces of those Wigan supporters will stay with me forever. A year later it happened for us.

August 26

Wigan. This was a place we felt we could get something, maybe our first away win. But we lose 1-0 and there is a feeling of disappointment because we really didn't do ourselves justice. Sometimes I reckon fans don't take into account how much travelling can affect performances, but we've had two away trips in a matter of days and I think it has taken something out of us. There is a very fine line between winning and losing and being

Emile Heskey rifles a shot past me for the only goal at Wigan.

American, I try to look for positives. But then Steve Coppell is as British as you can get and he always looks for positives too.

Lits almost scored in the last minute, but Chris Kirkland made a good save and last year we would probably have scored in that situation. That's the difference in the Premiership. We have to do what Manchester United and Chelsea do all the time and that's win when not playing well. Last year in the Championship we would have found a way of getting something from the game and nearly did this time had it not been for Kirkland.

Despite losing two of the first three matches, Steve Coppell is not one to panic.

August 27

I'm watching *Match of the Day* and all the experts are saying here at the end of August that we look like relegation candidates. I find it hard to take. Have they seen us play? How well do they know our players? Still, the stats do back them up. Two defeats in three is not the best of starts and against teams we fancied beating, but there is no despondency. The way we came back from two goals down to beat Middlesbrough gave us a belief that anything was possible. I shall make it my mission to prove those pundits wrong.

August 28

Sam Sodje made his debut against Wigan in place of Sonks. Sam is fantastic in the air. In Sweden I remember him heading the ball 75 yards. Goalkeepers like guys such as Sonks, Ivar and Sam because of their great heading ability, soaking up danger before it gets through to us. Sam has this strange habit of shouting 'Hi..ya' at the top of his voice as he jumps to head the ball. The guys do take the piss sometimes and shout 'Hi..ya' as well.

August 29

Reinforcements. Steve Coppell has brought in Ulysses de la Cruz from Aston Villa and Andre Bikey on loan from Moscow Lokomotiv. 'Dela' is from Uruguay and we soon get to call him 'El Presidente' and he seems to like it. Dela is a long way from home, but is aware of his good fortune and has not forgotten those he left behind. From his wages, he sends back ten per cent to family and friends in the little village in the mountains where he comes from. Bikey is Cameroonian and spent some time with us in Sweden so we could have a look about him. I think he's anxious to get away from Russia. He's strong and versatile and Steve Coppell like players who can play in more than one position. Bikey was sent off in Sweden in a friendly and Steve made it known that was not the Reading way, but he must have seen enough in him to bring him to England. I think there is some relief among our fans that we have made a couple of signings. Until de la Cruz and Bikey came in, we had brought in only two and they weren't household names. Our great rivals Sheffield United have been busier in the summer and there was some concern that our squad was not going to be deep enough.

August 30

The transfer deadline is tomorrow and we are wondering if Steve Coppell is going to pull off a big deal to see us through to January when the window opens for business again. Four months is a long time without being able to make signings and after the way we have started, it may seem like an eternity. But Steve is not one to panic. His last-minute business is confined to Peter Mate, a Hungarian midfield player on loan from Champions League club Debrecini. I guess that's the way we are and we have to get on with it. English players can be very expensive. Our total summer outlay is about £1.5 million, about the same as guys like Drogba and Schevchenko earned in the off season.

August 31

We have a free weekend coming up and it gives a chance to think about the three games gone and the 35 to come. At least I have my music to relax by. Seattle is steeped in rock music history. It was the home of Jimi Hendrix, Pearl Jam and Nirvana. I have been to Hendrix's graveside and we saw Pearl Jam at the Reading Festival. I have an electric guitar, but I'm bad at playing it. I don't have the patience to learn. I prefer to listen to those that can play, like Tool of course. I never tire of hearing Tool's '10,000 Days'. They are so passionate and energetic. Slipknot are another of my favourites, maybe a little harder and a bit more screaming than singing but this is the music I listen to before I go on to the pitch. I need something that pumps me up. The kids in the dressing room at Reading all play their R&B and it really irritates me. It doesn't get me excited or pumped up, but luckily that's what ipods were invented for and I can get away from it. I have hundreds of CDs and bits of music and have 107.5 days of it on my iPod. I guess it may be something to do with the fact that I'm older than some of the guys in the squad, but I feel sorry for them. Their music is crap.

SEPTEMBER

06

Time for the tough to get going.

September 4

We have a few days to gather our breath and our wits. There are internationals being played and we have lost a few players to them, so it's kind of strange at training without them. Sal Bibbo, our goalkeeping coach, tried to stop me feeling bad about the second Middlesbrough goal. Sal played for Reading and Sheffield United and is always there for me and the other goalkeepers. We don't always agree, but we discuss everything and have a good relationship. Sal is my biggest fan, he always backs me up when matches are analysed. Every keeper has strengths and weaknesses. My weakness, as you know, is my weight. I was skinny as a kid, but when I reached my teens, it became a problem. I tried other positions when I was growing up, but I first went in goal aged five, liked it, and settled there when I was about 14. Even then it was made clear to me that if you can't take the pressure, you should never go in goal. At some stage this season I know I will screw up. It's a fact. Every goal that goes past me I think and think again about why it did. Was I in the wrong position? Should I have been more positive? This is where Sal is so good, so reassuring.

My kicking technique.

All I can do is work my butt off in training with him. One of my strengths is my kicking and I like to think I can set up attacks that way, and with my throwing. My left foot is the weaker and Sal has me working on improving it all the time. Over the years I have got a lot better at my job. My hands are stronger, my decision-making is right many more times than it's not. Footwork is important. Goalkeepers are big guys and yet we need to be nimble these days since we can no longer pick up back passes. The problem for all of us keepers is the ball they now use. They are lighter, swirl in the air and change direction so that you can never be certain where they are going. That's why you see most of us punch the ball more than we did.

September 5

Our pitch is not the best in the Premiership. The rugby boys from London Irish use it as well, and I wonder what it will look like by the end of a long season. I don't like ruts and divots that get created by the Irish because I need to be sure about the surface when I'm kicking. When the ground is soft I don't kick as solidly as I would like. I expect one shank per game, and I get hammered by the rest of the team if my kicking is not up to standard. And Murty is the first to hammer me.

September 9

There is a full Premiership programme today, but our match with Manchester City doesn't take place until Monday evening. It's weird training on a Saturday when others are playing, but there is great anticipation because we will be on live Sky television and it's our chance to put right the disappointments of losing to Villa and Wigan.

September 10

I'm nursing a broken toe. A broken little toe on my right foot, to be exact, and it hurts more than I thought it would. (Six months later it still hurt). I collided with Shane Long in training, jumping for a cross and as we came down, he landed on my foot. I've had a lidocaine injection and there's no way I'm going to miss the Manchester City match. I have just got myself some new boots, but I can't put my swollen foot into them and feel comfortable. My old Nike boots are all I can wear for this one and I have to hope I don't worsen my toe during the game.

September 11

The plan is to replicate the way we played in the last hour against Middlesbrough, high tempo, aggressive and determined, in the way we won the Championship. It works. We win 1-0 and I don't think City can complain. Ivar Ingimarsson gets the winner. Ivar likes to go up for corners. He's a great header of the ball and this goal is real important. From my point of view it's my first Premiership clean sheet, a landmark for sure, in a super solid defensive performance. Last season, while we were being promoted we were happy to win 1-0 every game, if that was what we needed. We're beginning to work it out in the Premiership now.

Manchester City is a big club, we are not, but size doesn't matter. It means nothing. It's becoming clear to us that there are a lot of good teams in the Premiership but there is just as much inconsistency. Ivar hadn't scored since November, but we have learned a valuable lesson tonight. If you make mistakes at this level you will pay for it because there are so many quality finishers around. That was not always the case one step down. But the biggest thing, I think, is that for all the respect we must show our opponents there is nothing to be scared of.

Murts and me in the thick of the action against Man City.

September 13

Amanda writes.......

When we were in Germany for the World Cup, the antics of the English WAGs, as they came to be known, amused us all and made headlines in the English papers. They were in a different financial league to us, but no-one begrudged them having a good

The wives and girlfriends of Reading's players get together to form the Royals Families with the Reading Evening Post, a charity fundraising organisation aimed at helping two local charities, PACT (Parents And Teachers Together) and Berkshire Women's Aid.

time. I didn't know many of the wives and girlfriends of the American players, but I knew Bobby Convey's girlfriend and Eddie Lewis's wife. There was huge family support from both sets of our parents, Marcus's sister, her husband and their three children. Based, as we were in Hamburg, Artur organised everything because he knew the area so well. Marcus said he was going to be part of it, even if it meant carrying the bags, but I know how much he thrives on pressure and the bigger the stakes, the better he plays.

The wives and girlfriends of sports stars have a much higher profile in the United States than here in the UK. But not at all for the same reasons. I remember the Seattle Seahawks football team girls raising money for charity and I have often wondered why nothing similar happened in England. My parents, being educators, were not wealthy, but always gave money to charity and I grew up with that attitude. They even raised money for a Masai tribe in Kenya and I had felt for some time I would like to be involved in some kind of fund-raising initiative among the Reading wives and girlfriends. I mentioned it to Karen Murty, who has been a close friend, and before long the idea of the Royals Families began to take shape.

Reading is a friendly town, there was a lot of goodwill towards the football club after promotion and we started to make plans. I write a monthly column for the Reading Evening Post (I always fancied being a journalist) and Andy Murrell, the editor, and prime mover Hilary Scott were enthusiastic about our project. Andy West and Sara Jacob at the football club were also more than prepared to back us in terms of publicity and exposure. So today it all comes to fruition. Hilary, Karen and myself have chosen two charities on our doorstep. They are PACT (Parents And Teachers Together), which is about adoption, fostering and re-education, and Berkshire Women's Aid. This charity is about the consequences of domestic violence in the Reading area. They run a couple of drop-in centres, homes for abused women and single mothers. The Post is a very positive newspaper and their backing was much appreciated. Karen suggested the figure of £60,000 as a combined total to aim at, I think £10,000 is nearer the mark. I feel the big target at this stage might be a bit intimidating, but we are fortunate to have had as our aid, Sue Roberts, a special events manager. As our campaign progressed we would not have been able to do anything without her, she was that important. The club's sponsors, Kyocera, also got to hear what we were doing and leant their full support. So today we are up and away.

September 14

For the first time this season we are under pressure, or so I feel. This weekend we play Sheffield United and there is some feeling between us. They came up with us and are likely, according to the experts anyway, to be contesting relegation with us. That win over Manchester City has removed a little of the fear amongst our squad, but Sheffield are one of the teams likely to be in our 'league' or 'group' within the Premiership, so we must be positive when we go to Bramall Lane and stop them gaining anything at our expense.

There were always issues with Sheffield United when Alan Pardew was our manager and I guess it may have something to do with Neil Warnock. I happen to think Warnock is good for the game, but not everyone shares my view. Even when Pards left, the feeling continued.

September 15

We've played Sheffield United a lot over the years and they are a decent group of guys. We met them one time at the races at Cheltenham and we got on fine. Some of the players have been there a long, long time. I like Paddy Kenny, the goalkeeper, but Chris Morgan sums them up best. Morgan will smash into you at corners and free kicks, elbows and legs everywhere, and expects the same in return. With him it's a war, but there's no malice. Once against us he got laid out, but he just got up and got on with the game. What I like about him is that once the final whistle blows he shakes your hand and thanks you. What's done is done and I like guys like him. I hate things to spill over at the end. I remember once almost having a punch-up in the tunnel at Montreal when I was playing for Colorado Rapids, but Morgan is honest, gives nothing and expects nothing.

I've come across some aggressive strikers in my time, Stoke's Ade Akinbiyi and Gifton Noel-Williams have crashed into me in the past and I really felt it. I missed the last ten games of the 2003/04 season with cruciate ligament damage after a collision with Noel-Williams. But there was never any intention by him to hurt me and a keeper has to accept it. It's part and parcel of the job.

September 16

This was a big win for us. Doyle and Seol scored our goals in a 2-1 win, our first away from home in the Premiership, and we've put Sheffield United in their place for the time being. Kevin is showing he can score at this level and I'm pleased for Seol. He's had to join a group of players who have been together as a unit

Kevin Doyle opens the scoring in the first minute at Sheffield.

for a couple of years and it can't ever be easy trying to break into that. That's three wins out of our first five Premiership matches. Nine points out of 15. I think we would have taken that in the middle of August before a ball was kicked. But there are some major, major games coming up and we needed to make the start we have.

The celebrations of that opening goal
at Bramall Lane reach the fans.

September 18

There is an extra edge to training today. Manchester United are due at our stadium on Saturday and they don't come any bigger than United. I've waited all summer for this. No, all my career. United are one of the biggest clubs in the world and the thought of playing them as equals sends a tingle down the spine. When I was growing up in Seattle and I first became aware of big soccer clubs abroad, United were one of those who caught my imagination.

September 19

Graham Stack is my deputy, one of several players to come to us from Arsenal's youth academy. Tonight we play Darlington in the Carling Cup at home and I'm being rested. Stacky gets his chance and I'm on the bench. We give several of our squad players a game, guys like Peter Mate, John Halls, Ulysses de la Cruz, Andre Bikey, Brynjar Gunnarsson, John Oster and Shane Long. It's important we keep them involved. We are going to need them over the season. Lits scores twice, Mate gets the other, but we draw 3-3 and need penalties to get through. Ok, the Carling Cup is not a priority, but we want to win every game we play. I sit among the substitutes and every now and then the words Manchester and United drift into my mind.

September 21

Steve Coppell played for Manchester United, so this is bound to be special for him. But you would never know it. He's only interested in finding ways to beat them. Watch out for the long range shots of Paul Scholes and don't give Ronaldo any room, he tells us. We've seen them often enough on TV to know what to expect, but it's a timely reminder.

September 22

One day to go and the pressure is building. The papers are full of David versus Goliath, television crews haunt the training ground and I head for Ray's garage to get away from it all this Friday afternoon. I reckon if I hang out there for a few hours, fiddling with the Porsche, I can forget about Manchester United until I'm ready. But no, there's no escape. Ray's brother, Mike, comes bursting into the garage. The Manchester United bus has been spotted in town. The team bus.

In relaxed mood awaiting Manchester United.

September 23

This is it. Reading against Manchester United. The whole town has United fever and it's hard to ignore it or not to feel affected by it. But I see no reason to alter my home match-day routine. It's always the same. I get up at 9ish and Amanda makes sure the kids are super quiet. At their age, they can be loud, but they seem to know when I'm playing and make sure I'm not disturbed. I have a hot tub and then a breakfast of scrambled eggs and tons of coffee. For 30 minutes I lose myself in my Xbox. The Xbox comes with me to away games, too, that and my DVDs. Then I shower and, on match days, shave my head. It's an old ritual and I will explain why later, but that takes me to about mid-day and I'm ready to go.

Pangbourne is a quiet, gentle backwater and a world away from the Madejski Stadium, 24,000 plus people and the superstars of Manchester United. We have to be in place at 1.30 for a 3pm kick off, but I like to be there two hours before the start. I listen to Tool in the 20 minutes drive to the stadium and I can sense the tension building. Then it's time for lunch. Some players have pasta and beans or chicken, or whatever works for them. I'm probably the weirdest. I like a tuna sandwich and it must be canned tuna. I don't know why, but it's all part of the ritual, superstition or whatever you want to call it. Occasionally I will go for a variation, but not often and it has to be my idea. I like to be professional in everything I do and my rituals help me prepare, but it's mental as much as physical. I want everything to be the same. I know one or two players eat fish the night before the game, but not me.

For evening games there is a lot of hanging about and I like it less. I have to do something physical in the mornings, just to take my mind off the game ahead. I take Hunter and Austin on our bikes to school, anything to get out of the house. Sometimes I find a Starbucks for a coffee or two, but at that stage in the day I just need not to think about football. I rest for an hour in the afternoon and then have my tuna sandwich at 4pm. There is a pre-match meal for those who come in from a long distance, but most of the guys live in the Reading area now. I make no allowances in my schedule today just because Manchester United and their team bus are here.

Doyle puts us ahead from the penalty spot against Man U.

Later......

We draw 1-1. We could have won. Kevin Doyle put us ahead with a penalty and it needed a bit of magic from Ronaldo, cutting in from the left on to his right foot and shooting across me into the corner to deny us a famous victory. We treated it almost like a cup-tie and at the end we were almost disappointed not to win. Scholes is as dangerous as the gaffer said he would be and you just can't get the ball off Ronaldo. What surprised me was his strength and while we all know about his tricks, his step-overs, his pace and his shooting, I hadn't realised just how good he was in the air. He's just about the perfect player at the moment. We tried not to be overawed and I don't think we were. I was with Edwin van der Sar and Louis Saha at Fulham, so I was pumped up as soon as I knew they were in the team. It's a great point and I don't think I could have saved the goal. We go home content that we have already got many more points than we expected. United take it well, but you could see that they thought it was two points dropped.

Still later.....

I don't often stay behind after games, not even to have a beer or two with friends. Today is no different either. I go home and order our fish and chips, Chinese and Indian takeaways. While that's being done I pour myself a little drop of America, a Jim Beam bourbon with ice. I might have a second later, just to help relax, but that's all I ever want. I guess it's another little ritual. As I say, the house is always busy Saturday nights and there's plenty of food. Today has been special. We have just played Manchester United and got a good draw and it's another ambition fulfilled.

September 24

I wake up this Sunday morning with stud marks on my legs and arms. I know how it happened and who did it. There was a collision and my arms and legs were raked as several players tangled. I initially thought Kieran Richardson had done it, not deliberately, but painfully. It hurt bad. But then Murts kept asking me if I was all right. Again and again. Then it occurred to me why he was so concerned. "It was you, wasn't it?" I said when play was at the other end. For the rest of the match he kept apologising. I don't blame him in the least, but it's nice to hear him say he's sorry.

September 25

Back at training, the talk is still of Manchester United, even if the circus - and the team bus - has left. We are settling into the Premiership now and the back four which was unbelievable last year is again super solid. Had many people heard of Murts, Sonko, Ingimarsson and Shorey before this season? I'm pleased for Murts. He's been here since 1998, never played in the Premier League and will be 32 soon. I know he worried if he was going to be good enough at this level, but he's been fantastic from day one. I always knew he would be ok defending, though maybe going forward would be a problem. But Murts has gone forward and affected games as a good right-back should.

September 26

I love playing against West Ham. After Manchester United, this was the match I most looked forward to the moment I saw our fixtures. We have always had some super games with the Hammers and the fact that Alan Pardew is the manager of West Ham gives the game a whole new dimension. I also made what I consider to be my best ever save against West Ham from Jermain Defoe.

I have a lot to thanks Pards for. He gave me my chance. I had spent some time at Fulham and was going nowhere, except maybe home to America, until he brought me to Reading on loan. I had a great few years with Pards and he's polar opposite to Steve Coppell. Where Steve is quiet, considered and thoughtful, Pards is vocal and emotional. What he did for me most was give me confidence. At that stage of my career I was still a novice in terms of experience, a handful of games for Fulham was all I had to show for a year or two in England and I guess I needed someone to have some faith in me. Pards did that. He had this way of telling you that there was not a better goalkeeper in the world, and I might just have believed him. But I remember once him hammering me at half-time, saying that if I didn't do as he told me, he would get someone who would. You could tell the score by his reactions on the pitch-side and for those of us who have played for both managers, Steve Coppell is not so easy to read. Pards could be funny off the pitch, as can Steve, who has a dry sense of humour. Pards could be odd as well. He introduced some annoying rules, like not being allowed to wear baseball caps on the team coach. But it will be good to see him again.

September 28

We don't play at West Ham until Sunday, which means another blank Saturday, something we need to get used to. In the Championship we played almost all our games on Saturday, but in all ways it's a different world in the Premiership. I use my free Saturday to hang out with my wife and children. Among the players we don't live in each other's pockets. Golf is the common denominator. I have a handicap of ten and there are some good

Relaxing in the garden with the boys.

golfers among us. The Irish boys, Bobby Convey, Murts, Shorey, Hallsy and Stacky are all naturally competent. Blakey is very good. Federici and Bibbo are regular golfing partners of mine. No other player shares my interest in cars, so my closest friends in England are people like Ray Northway, while the fact that I'm a family man and older than many removes me from the nightclub scene where the younger guys go. I'm at a different stage of my life. But it's good to do things as a team and golf unites us. Stacky won the club competition, but I'm not sure about his true handicap. Stacky would cheat his mum. Much as I love golf, it takes a toll these days. My left hip hurts me more and more and I don't want to do anything which might mean me dropping out of the team.

September 29

Playing golf gave me one of my nicknames, Red Bird. I got that from the international team. I can hit a ball a long, long way if I get it right. One day I pulled from my bag this Red Bird driver and drove it miles. I think it was Pablo Mastroeni who saw me reaching into my bag one day and warned the others: "Look out, here comes Red Bird." For a time it stuck. Another nickname was 'Boomer'. When I was at Fulham I asked the guys what name we should give our newly-born second child Austin and Paul Peschisolido suggested 'Boomer'. But among the Reading players, I'm 'Buddy'. English people tend to say 'mate' when addressing someone. Being American I say Buddy. Whatever.

September 30

The years in England are getting to me. I start referring to the car trunk as the boot, as you say here. Then one day I ask for a cheese and tomarto pizza. Amanda almost died laughing and has never let me forget it. Still, as the old song goes, I say tomayto, you say tomarto.

Meanwhile.......

We play West Ham tomorrow at Upton Park and after our success against Manchester United, Steve Coppell has been preaching the need for caution, not to be carried away by what we have achieved so far. We may have exceeded expectations, even those of ourselves, but this is the last day of September and there are eight months to go. He's right, of course. I know he and Pards are quite close, which gives the game a little something extra. Steve has this incredible ability to pinpoint exactly where a match could be won and lost. We discuss the opposition on Friday afternoons for Saturday matches and he would say, for instance, the key area is going to be the wings and just about every time he has read it perfectly. He's well briefed, of course, but from my position in goal I can see a match unfolding in just the way he says it would.

Will he be right tomorrow? My guess is he will.

SEPTEMBER 06

MARCUS HAHNEMANN'S PREMIERSHIP DIARY

OCTOBER

Making a point.

06

October 1

It's a Sunday afternoon, we are playing West Ham at Upton Park and it's raining. There is a rain storm as we warm up and when the match starts there is a big puddle in my goalmouth. It makes me nervous. I dread what might happen if a shot is driven into that water, and, of course, there is one almost immediately. It skips through and then sticks, drenching me. But there's no goal.

You could see even then that it wasn't going right for Pardew or his team. It would have hurt him losing to us. We didn't want him to move to West Ham and our chairman contested it, but he left in the end to further his ambition. Now he's been beaten by the team he left behind. This was a big away win for us, bigger than winning at Sheffield United. Sheffield are contemporaries, so that was us putting them in their place. Winning at West Ham was different because they are a famous club and established in the Premiership. Bobby Convey and Seol set up the goal at a free-kick. Bobby decided to play it short to Seol and I was annoyed. Seol was keyed up for a shot and I reckoned it was going to be a waste from that distance. But he struck it perfectly high into the top corner. What do I know? We win again and Sky TV record it live. I can't get used to being on television so much.

October 3

Training is fun these days. We've picked up 13 points out of a possible 21 and we have to be happy with that. My daily training routine is almost as rigid as it is for match days, but not quite. I'm up at 8.30, spend ten minutes loosening up in the hot tub and easing that problem left hip. It sucks. The hip is sore and I wonder if it gets bad enough I will need surgery.

I take Hunter and Austin to school on their bikes and then it's Slipknot and Tool in the car on the way to the training ground. The keepers start at about 10.15am, before the outfield players, in the gym. There are ropes, bikes, rowing machines. Some guys do the weights, but not me. I don't want my muscles to get tired. Sal Bibbo keeps an eye on all of us keepers, even the 16 year-olds. We work on stretching, our handling and our feet. I don't like changes and I prefer my preparations to resemble those on match

A goalkeeper's life can be a lonely one.

days. Then we practice volleys, half volleys, anything to test reactions and movement and the young lads follow what we do.

October 4

I can accept criticism from Sal and, as I say, we analyse my performances together, but I get touchy when others criticise me. I tell them to f*** off. They can have no idea. I get defensive if outfield players make a comment about me, or the way I've played. I can just about take it from any of the back four, but even then I'm prepared to argue my case. I guess it's because goalkeepers are so confidence-orientated and you don't want to hear anything that causes doubts. Making decisions is the hardest part, but I reckon that 99 times out of 100 if I come for the ball I get something on it. There are always decisions to be made. Should I catch? Should I punch? If I make the wrong one, it's obvious and in my position it can be costly. If Sal tells me I got it wrong, I listen.

October 5

No match now for another couple of weeks due to internationals. Then it's Chelsea, Arsenal and Liverpool in the league and Liverpool in the Carling Cup, but I think Stacky will be in for that one. All of us have noted a big difference between the Premiership and the Championship in the seven matches we have played so far. The players are bigger, faster, stronger. They pass it around much more. If you can't pass, you won't survive. The level of skill is fantastic. The way some of these guys control the game is incredible and the passing even under pressure is phenomenal. Manchester United were ridiculously good, the timing of the runs, the weight of pass. It was a joy to watch even if we were on the receiving end rather than enjoying it on the box. Another thing I have noticed, the pitches around the Premiership are far better than ours. The middle of our pitch is not holding up. Some of our guys say we 'launch' the ball too much, but this can be a strength. I reckon I'm at the start of many of our goals, but I know I need to throw more to get us going forward at pace.

October 13

We are about to enter a key phase. All these big teams coming at us in a wave. I find it incredibly exciting. Luckily we have some points in the bag already and the confidence to go with it. The crowds are mega big, home and away. That causes a problem for me. I can't hear what team-mates are saying and the rest of the team struggles to hear my instructions. The defence has to be able to hear what I'm shouting otherwise there can be chaos. When I was a kid I had a temper and over the years I have developed a loud voice. In the Championship the guys in front of me could hear every word. It's not so easy now with all that noise.

My loud voice goes home with me. One time I frightened a neighbour's wife when I raised it. She was almost crying.

October 14

I was looking forward to facing Chelsea today. They are the champions and have an endless list of outstanding players.

We lost 1-0, but the match will always be remembered for the injuries to Petr Cech and the other Chelsea goalkeeper Carlo Cudicini. I feel sorry for Stephen Hunt. This is Hunty's first game of the season and was his big chance. But within minutes his knee collided with Cech's head and the place took off. Let's get this right from the start, Hunty did not mean to hurt Cech. He's an energetic lad and he was chasing down a possible opening. There was no malice, he's not that type of guy. It was an awkward challenge at worst, but these things happen. It could easily have happened to me. But because it's Chelsea the incident takes on a life of its own. As for Cudicini, I didn't see it at the time. I was in

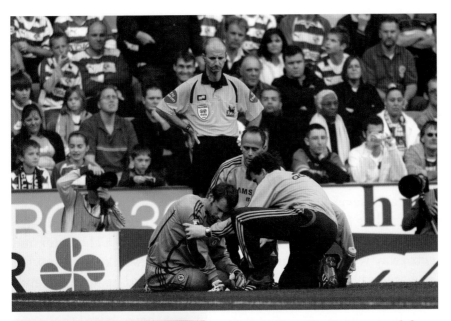

Above, Petr Cech is treated for his injury and left, John Terry replaces Carlo Cudicini.

the Chelsea box at a corner, looking for an equaliser with time running out when he crashed into Sonks. Now believe me, you do not want to collide with Sonks. He's got to be the strongest man in the world and, if you get hit by him, you'll know about it.

I see it later on television and Sonks is already in the air when the collision occurs. No way was that intentional. Sonks doesn't carry an ounce of fat. Me? I just have to look at a banana to put on weight. As for Hunty, I say nothing to him about what happened because it was an accident. But you could see he was upset.

Later....

Only when I switch on *Match of the Day* do I realise just how big all this is. Jose Mourinho seems to have over-reacted. He is openly criticising our club, Hunt, even the Berkshire ambulance service. His outburst is unbelievable. I know it's his job to protect and stand up for his players, but this is crazy. Okay, to lose two goalkeepers in the same match to concussion is incredible and he's obviously worried. But the Hunt incident is shown again and again and never looks any more deliberate.

I like Mourinho. Football in this country needs people like him, that's what makes the game great here. He's a character and gets away with being controversial. Most times I like to hear what he has to say. After all, it's only his opinion and he always stands by his players. I respect that. But I can't help thinking that if this had been Spurs, say, there would not have been the same controversy. It's magnified beyond belief because it's Mourinho and Chelsea.

October 16

Training. Hunty is not his normal self. Most days he's one of the liveliest and bubbliest, but not today. He's super quiet, which is very unlike him. No-one says anything to him. He's got nothing to be ashamed of and will recover in time, but I think the Chelsea game has affected us all. We are not a dirty side and never have been in all my time here. Steve Coppell would never sign any player with a bad disciplinary record and discourages any kind of dissent. But we have been made out to be the villains in the papers, as if we had gone out to maim the Chelsea goalkeepers.

October 17

The amount of publicity the Chelsea match has generated has stunned us. It just goes on and on. We are new to the Premiership and new to the kind of relentless scrutiny it brings. Fresh from the Championship, we are not used to it and it's hard to take. Having a go at us about the slowness of our ambulance service was pretty low, especially as I think it's simply because they struggled to beat us and I think we will be glad when it all finally blows over.

October 19

Goodbye Chelsea, hello Arsenal. It doesn't get any easier. I like watching Arsenal and Thierry Henry is one of my favourite players.

    Steve Coppell is as positive as ever and raises our spirits as the match day approaches. He must have sensed we needed it. And we do have to be positive. We drew with Manchester United and lost to Chelsea only by a single goal.

October 22

Another Sunday match, and this time we get a thrashing. We are a goal down in a minute or two and you just can't do that against a team like Arsenal. Steve Coppell said that whatever we did, not to concede an early goal, it being harder to get back than if we were playing Manchester United and Chelsea. We were never in it, as 4-0 would indicate. We can't complain. I almost admired the way they passed the ball around. This is the first time we have been blown apart, no other team has done that to us. I guess our fans suddenly realise what league we are in. Henry is hard to read. He spends long quiet periods, doing nothing, and then he flies, that awesome mixture of pace, power and skill. I didn't get near his penalty that made it 4-0.

Action from the thumping we received by Arsenal.
Above: I bring down Fabregas for one of the penalties.
Below: Van Persie slots home Arsenal's third.

We come off, wondering what the manager is going to say. As usual he puts it into sensible perspective. "It does not matter. It does not make or break us. It does not define us."

October 23

Arsenal keeper Jens Lehmann is a super nice guy. Gunners fans love him, but around England, and maybe Germany, they don't appear to like him as much as I do. I sat with him in the Arsenal dressing room for a chat after the game and we got along fine. Graham Stack was with him at Arsenal and said he was crazy off the pitch. He's an extrovert who also loves a bit of controversy on the pitch to get him going. I can understand that. With him there's always something going on. Remember when Jens and Didier Drogba kept knocking each other over? Great.

    I reckon there's a Jens Lehmann you see, and another you don't. As a goalkeeper, I admire him. He makes brilliant saves and has played in some big matches all over the world, including in the World Cup semi-final back in July.

October 24

The reason I went to see Jens was to get his shirt. I collect them. For the first seven matches I decided I would not go up to the opposition's keeper and ask for their shirts because I did not want people to think we are happy just to be in the Premier League, but with Jens it was different and he happily handed it over. As for my own shirts that's another story I'll tell you about later. Now, after seven games we appear to be holding our own.

October 25

Steve Coppell's policy is to give reserve and fringe players a game in the non-Premiership matches. That means I'm on the bench at Liverpool for tonight's Carling Cup game. We lose 4-3 and there's a super exciting last 20 minutes as we threaten a surprise. I get far more excited on the sidelines than I do when I'm playing. I can lose my temper on the bench, booing what I think are bad refereeing decisions.

October 28

We are at Portsmouth. It's a crazy place to go. I was there once with Fulham, so I know what to expect. They have an old stadium, but their fans are terrific and they have some great players. Kanu is unbelievable and has had an amazing start to the season. He holds everything up front and brings other players into the game more

It's an own goal from Gunnarsson at Fratton Park.

deftly than he has a right to do with his size 18 feet. Kanu's first touch is fantastic for such a big guy. It's a poor performance from us. We lose 3-1 and we are as soundly beaten as we were by Arsenal. It sucks. Two bad results and bad performances in six days.

Portsmouth are flying and play with a lot of confidence. After years of merely avoiding relegation, they are talking about Europe already. A point would have done us.

It's strange to see an uncovered stand at this level. The atmosphere would be even better with a roof on it. But I don't feel intimidated, not like I was at Wigan where fans running on to the pitch took all my clothes except my shorts, or at Burnley a couple of years ago when a plastic bottle of Coke just missed my head. Here we let in an early goal, as we had done against Arsenal, and we go home worried that our season may be falling apart. It will, if we play like this again.

October 30

Those shirts of mine. At the end of each match I throw my shirt among our fans behind or near the goal. Another ritual, I guess. It all began in my second year with Reading on the anniversary of September 11 and the twin towers. A guy in the crowd waving an American flag asked for my shirt and, patriotically, I threw it to him. The following Monday I got a letter from a prominent member of the backroom staff saying I was not at Fulham now and would have to pay for it. That just made me more determined to do it again. So over the next few games I was buying them from the club shop and throwing them into the crowd and the whole thing began to escalate. Two weeks later I got another letter, this time from Boyd Butler in the marketing department in which he said the feedback they were getting from fans was great. As a special concession he would sell them to me at cost price. It was clear to me also that our supporters were looking to me to throw the shirts at them and I thought it a small price to pay considering my salary and bonuses. The growth in American flags was noticeable and the clamour became greater by the match. One

Those famous Hahnemann shirts - paid for in full by Kyocera!

time I got booed and it was all a misunderstanding. I had been asked to give my shirt to a handicapped child in the disabled section at the Madejski Stadium. I passed it to a steward to do it for me and the fans thought I had given it to him as a present. Then they noticed he was giving it to the child and the boos turned to cheers.

That's the way it was until our sponsors, Kyocera, stepped in. They are now sponsoring my shirts this year, so I can keep giving them away. The reason I do all this is that Reading fans have been great to me over the years and it's my way of thanking them for taking me to their hearts so readily from the moment I arrived, pretty much unknown. Maybe it's because I'm an American, but I never take anything like that for granted. Even when we were getting 14,000 crowds when I first came, not the 24,000 we now get in the Premier League, I wanted to show how much I appreciated the support I got.

October 31

We come to the end of one hell of a month. It began in the rain at West Ham, continued with Chelsea and Mourinho and ended with poor performances against Arsenal and Portsmouth. We are learning fast. The Premiership is everything we hoped and feared it would be, but there is no loss of confidence or desire to improve. We have had a crazy run of big clubs and only Arsenal have exposed any kind of gap in class. We are still 'little Reading' in the papers, but that doesn't annoy us. I think they all believe that over a ten-month season we will go down, but there's no way we share that view. In many ways being called 'little' does us a favour. Some of our opponents might continue to underestimate us and that suits us fine.

MARCUS HAHNEMANN'S PREMIERSHIP DIARY

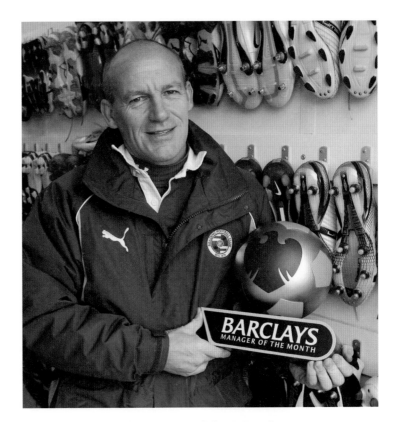

NOVEMBER

06

Manager of the Month.

November 1

I'm a fierce American patriot. I love my country, even to the extent of having the United States flag, the stars and stripes, tattooed on my left shoulder. I got it done at Fulham in 2000 just to annoy the other guys. Paul Peschisolido, a Canadian, had a go at me and said not all 50 stars were on it. For that to happen, it would have to have been all over my back.

Amanda and I have been in England a long time now and we love it where we are. But when we first came to London and were living in Wimbledon we were struck by how hard it was to strike up casual conversations in the street, even with people we had seen before. But it's different out here in our village. You get stopped all the time; everyone wants to chat. In fact it's so nice, you can be late for training that way. Another thing which struck us straight away was the news coverage. In America, the press tends to show the United States in a good light, but in Europe there is much more spin in the newspapers, sometimes it seems to me, against America. In England the press is much more critical of our government and other governments, as well as their own. The Iraq war is an example, I guess. But I'm not offended. Criticism is healthy and part of democracy.

November 2

I'm looking forward to this month. We go back to Liverpool for a league match, so hopefully I will get to play at Anfield, Tottenham come to the Madejski and, at the end, we play my old club Fulham. I didn't play much first team football there, but they gave me a step into English football and I will always be grateful for that. My path to Reading has been kind of strange. I had been playing at Seattle Sounders when I got this chance to double my money and move up to the MLS with Colorado Rapids. I think both Amanda and I were ready to try our luck elsewhere and I know she was happy and excited about living in another part of the United States. I was starting to get a reputation. I had played for the United States in three internationals in 1994 and 1995 as a Seattle player against Trinidad and Tobago, Jamaica and Honduras. I didn't kid myself. Guys like Kasey and Brad Friedel were being rested for bigger matches ahead. To play for your country is a fantastic feeling and, while it didn't rate much coverage in the papers back home, it whetted the appetite.

All the while I was going to England when I could for trials with clubs, brandishing my German passport. But while I was waiting for Europe to happen, Colorado came in for me and off we went. The MLS was beginning to get a profile, the standard of play was undoubtedly better than I had been used to, and teams were stronger. It was kind of weird in those days in America in that while the MLS was the best place to be, not all the country's best players were in it. The A league still had a core of very capable footballers and the indoor leagues were also thriving. They were almost competing for the best players. I may have stepped up a level, but it was another eight years, five months and 28 days before I was chosen again for the national side. That must be some kind of record.

Amanda writes.......

I was getting fed up with being a personal trainer and Colorado sounded good. Marcus had got in the national side, but he needed to push himself out of the comfort zone. It would have been too easy to stay in Seattle. We kept in touch with Paul Barron and we had a look at West Ham, Villa and Stuttgart. It was always in the back of our minds that we would go over to Europe eventually.

Paul and Chris encouraged Marcus to keep at it and told him what he must do. I think he learned a lot from them about what was required to be a professional goalkeeper. When we first arrived in Colorado I wondered if we had made the right move. I looked out of the airplane window and there wasn't a tree or water in sight. But we came to love the sunshine and water skiing. We loved the sunshine and the winter skiing. Marcus is a great skier and was an instructor. One of the drawbacks of being a full-time footballer is that skiing is off the agenda for him at the moment. But the outdoor lifestyle was great, our favourite was camping in the mountains.

Marcus's sister got me a good job with a wholesale mortgage company. We had a busy social life among the other Rapids players, many of whom lived in the same apartment block. We were finally making money. In fact, I think I was earning more than Marcus. Before we left for England three years later in 1999, Hunter was born, so we were very happy and well set. But at the back of our minds, we were still ambitious and willing to in vest in his soccer future.

Signing shirts in the club shop.

November 4

Peter Crouch is so big and stronger than you think. I know he can look ungainly, being so tall, but his touch is great and he's a real problem for goalkeepers and defenders. People said to me he's better on the ground than in the air, but you could have fooled me. Being 6 ft 7 inches, four inches taller than me for a start, he just seems to hang there in the air making it awkward to stop him. He can jump too and has this great ability to get into position early. I may be stating the obvious, but here at Anfield today he looks a formidable player. We lose 2-0 and Dirk Kuyt gets both the goals, but it's Crouch who catches the eye. Anfield is a great stadium and it's weird going back to it so soon after sitting on the bench there in the Carling Cup, but in terms of a result it's not getting any better for us.

I knew Steve Finnan, the Liverpool full-back, at Fulham and we were good friends until we went our separate ways. Steve is a class right-back and, I think, a little underrated. While it's good to see Steve again, this is our fourth league defeat in a row, fifth if you include losing here in the Carling Cup, and it's not a comfortable ride home.

November 5

Sure enough the papers are all saying the same thing. The Reading bubble has burst. Not just the papers. One or two of our fans probably feel the same way. Four in four says it all. But Steve Coppell is not downhearted and nor are we. We have lost to Chelsea, Arsenal, Portsmouth and Liverpool. Only at Portsmouth would we have reasonably expected to get a point. What a sequence of matches. Only Arsenal truly thumped us and overall we have played a lot of really good football, even in defeat. There is no getting away from the fact that we have played against some great teams and they have shown us why they are so good and what it takes to compete with them. We knew as soon as the fixtures came out that this was going to be a super tough period, so while there is some sense of doom around and about, none of us, the Reading players, are paying any attention to it.

November 6

Throughout the world international appearances are known as receiving a cap. It's common knowledge and a common term. One day at Fulham, Maik Taylor showed me one that he had got playing for Northern Ireland. It really was a cap with a peak and a tassle. We don't have anything like that in America and it was a bit of a surprise to actually see one.

November 9

We need to beat Tottenham because a draw is not much use to us. But let's get it in perspective, how many teams win at Liverpool? We still have 13 points, five more than Newcastle and there are some big clubs below us. If we stick together we'll come through this, but we have had a tough run. It's really important we get three points from this game.

November 11

For me the Tottenham match has an extra personal edge. Amanda's cousin, Kelly, married a hige Spurs fan, Stephen. They live in London and Kelly is almost as much a Spurs fans as he is. I've got him a ticket in the away end - Kelly is with Amanda - and I hope we can ruin his afternoon.

Stephen and Kelly Hollingworth - the Tottenham fans.
Kelly is Amanda's cousin.

November 12

Another Sunday match. Tottenham are a team filled with great talent, but we beat them 3-1. Shorey, Sidwell and Doyle score our goals and there is a sense of relief in the dressing room afterwards because we have proved a lot to ourselves and to other people. I'm pleased for Nick Shorey. Nick is super steady; he just never makes mistakes. Funny I should mention Finnan recently because Nick reminds me of him in many ways. He's not big, but he's good in the air and has this ability to get into position early and uses his body. Kevin Davies at Bolton, incidentally, is best at that in my view. Nick is quick and is our cross leader, his set play delivery is unbelievable and he seems to be relishing the bigger stage the Premiership has provided him. Not that he ever talks about himself or pumps himself up. He's quiet and modest and gets on

Above: Steve Sidwell scores the second
of our three against Spurs.
Below: I save at point blank range from Hossam Ghaly.

with his job. Spurs are a big team, laden with talent, but they don't have the best of away records. This result has got us back to where we want to be and it has given us a great boost at just the right time.

Later that evening.......

Stephen is the most miserable man you have ever seen. "Don't say anything," he pleads as I come into the players' bar. I can't kick a man when he's down, but it's hard to resist. Kelly has wound him up and he's been forced to admit Reading deserved to win. And so we did.

November 14

Martin Jol, the Tottenham manager, is quoted as saying that if you lose to Reading, you know you're right in trouble. His words are cut out and stuck on the notice board at the training ground, but there is no anger, only laughter. We have just beaten his team, but the words stay there for extra motivation.

As I see it, other Premiership managers will be thinking the same as Jol, it's just that he's gone ahead and said it out loud. I'm pretty certain that when the fixtures came out, there was hardly a manager in the land who didn't see six points

Martin Jol looking as devastated as Stephen Hollingworth did after the game - Jol's post-match comments served as extra motivation for us.

against our name, especially the bigger clubs like Spurs. It doesn't make us feel inferior, or even upset. Let's face it, teams like Tottenham cost millions to put together and to lose to us, little Reading, must be a real setback. There is no way we should be able to compete with Tottenham and Manchester United and others, but we are doing it the moment. We keep beating teams with far greater talent, player for player, but our success comes with the fact that we compete individually and as a unit.

November 15

I have begun talks with the Reading management about a new contract. Mine runs out at the end of the season and a footballer's life is dogged by insecurity. Glen Little and Graeme Murty are two other stalwarts of the promotion side who have proved they can handle the Premiership, but, like me, they are the wrong side of 30 and we all wonder if we are going to be replaced somewhere along the line. I guess the club needed to be sure we can cope with a big step up and I like to think we all have. I feel as though I'm on trial. Ideally I want a contract for life, to take me through to the natural end of my career, but in all honesty I can't see that happening.

November 16

I'm crazy for the *Star Wars* films. I was about six or seven when the first came out and I was hooked. I've seen the movies again and again. As a kid I collected all the cards. Now my kids love it too and we enjoy the films as a family. That's why I loved dressing up as Obi-Wan Kenobi before the recent United game (ready to take on the Fergie 'Empire'!) for one of the tabloid newspapers because they knew of my devotion to *Star Wars*. But, best of all, I have a signed photograph from the guy who played Boba Fett. He's a Tottenham fan and the inscription read: "To the Hahnemann family from the best centre-forward in the galaxy."

May the force be with me.

November 17

We are at home to Charlton tomorrow and it's the first time we have been expected to win since we were promoted. Charlton are

Defensive coach Wally Downes in cheerful mood.

a little like us, a small club trying to compete with the big boys and this season they're suddenly struggling after many years of honourable survival. Steve Coppell knows we must show them no mercy. In training, he stresses how we must beat them. To do that, he has instructed us to get at them from the kick-off. The gaffer has pointed out how this could be a banana skin because, while they might be lower in the table than us, they still have some quality players. If we give them no chance to settle there will be no chance for them to build a little confidence. Wally Downes is our defensive coach and he goes over our tasks for tomorrow. My job is to kick the ball down the left side, as far as possible, into the stands if

necessary, as long as it's deep into Charlton territory. Steve and Kevin Dillon have spotted a weakness there. Sometimes kicking the ball down the pitch can be self-defeating if some monster heads it back 70 yards. After our defensive meeting, the whole team gets together and we go over the key points. The message is simple, make sure there are no mistakes at the back and play the game in the Charlton half.

November 18

Three more points and a clean sheet. I could get used to this. Seol and Doyle score our goals in a 2-0 win and you can see Charlton are not happy. It's not working out for them yet, in the way it wasn't working out for Alan Pardew when we won at West Ham.

The plan works perfectly. We produce a great tempo from the first whistle and Charlton never get an opportunity to threaten. That's two home wins in succession and the worry caused by losing four in a row is being removed. I think today we know we are good enough to stay up.

November 20

Amanda writes.......

Today champagne corks are popping because we are launching our series of fund-raising events on behalf of our chosen charities at the Madejski Stadium. We are all a little nervous since none of us know if it will be a success, but it goes well. Tickets at £50 each allow the buyer to taste six different champagnes, there's canapés, an auction and a raffle. The Reading footballers mingle among our guests and with the considerable help and expertise of Sue Roberts, a professional special events manager, we raise a staggering £25,000, more than I had dared hope. Kyocera, the club's sponsors, are quick to back us, which gives us a royal seal of approval, after hearing of our intentions.

Karen and I are now joined in the Royals Families by Emily Bailey (Nicky Shorey's future wife), Olga Einarsdottir (Gunnarsson), Krystell Sidwell, Joanne Doyle (Stephen Hunt's girlfriend), Hrefna Arnardottir (Ingimarsson), Jenny Harney (Kevin Doyle's girlfriend), Sophie Hall (Leroy Lita), Claire Hollowell (Dave Kitson), Sarah Annesley (Shane Long), Sarah Little, Marina Bikey and Michaela, Adam Federici's girlfriend. Karen has been upbeat and proactive from day one, but all these other girls were quick to join our quest and we were surprised and delighted just how much interest has been generated and how much support we are receiving from businesses. Sue Roberts got us three gold sponsors, but having Kyocera back us so wholeheartedly was a bonus. I shall quote Tracey Rawling of Kyocera: "Kyocera are very pleased to establish a strong relationship with the Royals Families and help them continue the excellent work they have started. The activities they are involved with will make a difference to people's lives in Berkshire and we look forward to supporting them in the future."

November 21

Eddie Johnson is with us. Eddie was a member of the USA World Cup squad and is over here having a look at us, just as we are having a look at him. Eddie has noted how Bobby Convey and myself have settled in and are doing okay. He's a good kid and wants to learn. He plays up front and maybe Steve Coppell will like him enough to sign him, but there's plenty of competition. I know he wants to play in England, joining the ever-growing number of Americans who are making a living out of football in this country. Steve will be honest with him when the time comes to make a decision. I know he likes guys with something to prove and he won't be expensive by European standards.

November 23

Today is Thanksgiving Day, a major event in the American calendar and we take it seriously in our house. I spend an hour or two wandering around supermarkets looking for canned pumpkin fo the making of pumpkin pie. The English don't go in for it like we do at home, but pumpkin pie is essential for Thanksgiving and the good news is I find some. We cook two 17 pound turkeys and pumpkin pies and pecan pies, ten in total I think, because this is going to be a big feast. My sister, her husband and children are over, as is Amanda's uncle and family.

We are cooking for 32 and that's way too many for the house we live in. We have hired a room at our local Italian restaurant and once the food is cooked at home we take it down there. Many of our neighbours are joining us, honorary Americans for the night, and Eddie Johnson will be there of course, although Bobby Convey is in America getting some treatment on an injury. I like the stuffing for the turkeys.

The whole family in London in November. We had a lot of our folks out from the States for Thanksgiving.

November 24

It's going to be strange going back to Craven Cottage tomorrow. I had never heard of Fulham when they started showing some interest in me while I was playing for Colorado Rapids. We were half-way through an MLS season in July 1999 when Paul Bracewell, then manager at Fulham, came over to watch me in

New York. He was probably doing some shopping as well, but it just so happened that I had an incredibly busy match. We had a man sent off after ten minutes and I made tons of saves and held crosses from all directions. Two days later, on a Monday, I was playing golf when I got a call from my then agent. In the MLS all players are registered with the league and not the individual clubs. My agent said Fulham had agreed a fee of £85,000 with the MLS and I was to get over to England on Friday. I was on my way. Not even my club knew about it.

Amanda writes......

Marcus in effect just came home, grabbed a suitcase and fled. It may all have been a bit sudden, but I too was itching for a change. "Let's go," I said. I loved travelling anyway. I had lived in Guam for three years while my mom was teaching and dad was studying at the university and later I remember the fun I had snorkelling in Mexico and the Caribbean.

The timing of Marcus's transfer was not brilliant in one respect. There was a big Rapids game scheduled for July 4, a sell out in fact, with fireworks afterwards to celebrate Independence Day, but, of course, Marcus had gone. The Rapids coach, Glen 'Mooch' Myernick, later assistant coach to the national side and who died aged about 52, was unhappy about the way the MLS had sold Marcus to Fulham without his knowledge. But he always knew it was our ambition to go to England if the opportunity arose, and now it had.

We had just bought our first house in Colorado and now I had a very short time to pack up and leave. First thing I had to do was get rid of the motor sump oil Marcus had left behind in the garage. Then my dad, myself and our dog got in the Jeep that was more suited to rough terrain than main roads and drove and drove some more across the wide open spaces of America to Seattle. The journey seemed to take days and it was very hot. Meanwhile, my mother and baby Hunter, then about eight months old, had flown home and met us when we finally got there. Then it was on to London and a whole new world.

November 25

I think when Fulham let me go three years after I arrived they thought that I was not going to be good enough to be a Premiership goalkeeper. They had signed Edwin van der Sar after promotion and Maik Taylor was now main back-up. Two top class keepers. To that extent I believe I have proved a lot of people wrong. I'm playing in the Premiership regularly for Reading and I think also I'm much improved.

I find it to be a great experience going back. I had never set foot in Craven Cottage since I left until today, so I was not sure what to expect. There are still some familiar faces, Nigel and Bob the security men, the kitman, the physios. They all remember me. The backroom staff seems to be intact, but on the playing side only Boa Morte and Zat Knight have survived.

I'm wondering what sort of reception I'm going to get from the Fulham fans, but I needn't have worried. I get a good round of applause from the home end and I think they are pleased to see me back and what I've achieved since I left. I didn't leave on bad terms and there are no hard feelings from me towards their club. I was just unwanted and that happens in football all the time. Chris Coleman, the Fulham manager, was a close friend and playing colleague when I was there and we exchange a bit of banter. Chris is under pressure anyway, so he's in for a miserable Saturday evening after we win 1-0. Kevin Doyle scores the winner from the penalty spot and I go home delighted with another away win, another clean sheet, but with no sense of revenge satisfied. I wish Fulham no harm.

November 26

Fulham's Brian McBride asked how Thanksgiving dinner was and if we had as full a house as he did. I played against him in the MLS when he was with Columbus Crew. We speak on the phone occasionally and I am not surprised he has done well in England. He's one of the best leapers in the game and a powerful header.

The team celebrate Kevin Doyle's goal at Fulham.

I guess some people are surprised Kevin Doyle is taking our penalties, being so young and inexperienced, but he's not scared of the responsibility and we trust him. There's a difference between self-confidence and arrogance. Kevin is confident in his ability and expects to succeed when he's taking a penalty. When self-confidence is used negatively, it becomes arrogance, but Kevin is a level-headed guy and it's good to see someone wanting to step up under pressure.

November 27

I figure my trial period is over because today I am signing a new contract. Blakey [Glen Little] and Murts have got one as well. None of us have been on great money. Once we got into the Premiership, I guess people thought we would be paid huge sums.

But that is not the case. There are no big earners at Reading. All any of us wanted was to be paid what we were worth, a decent living to reflect the fact that we were now in the Premiership and doing okay. More than okay, in fact.

I hoped we would get new contracts the moment we were promoted and the longer it went without anything being said, the more fearful we all became. I felt we were being unnecessarily delayed and not being properly rewarded for our efforts. It was as if they didn't rate us. But today the club have finally recognised our contributions in getting the club into the Premiership and making such a good start. I think I shall be able to send some money home, save a bit, but that's only fair. The club is making a colossal amount just by being at this level and I for one was a little surprised that they were hesitant to acknowledge what we had done. Sure, there were questions about all of us. Many people thought we would go down and even at the end of November, still reckon it could happen. It's clear Reading thought: "Let's see if these guys are good enough, let them prove themselves."

In my view, what we lack in skill we make up for in heart. But there was no denying there was tons of pressure on all of us. Even now what I'm getting is a pay-as-you-go-contract, based on appearances, clean sheets, wins and draws. I have to play 20 games in 2007/08 to get another year's contract, but I'm all for incentives. The whole business was done quickly. The agent who got me to England has long been history and I use the PFA to help me with negotiations. Nigel Howe, our chief executive at Reading, is a reasonable man and the club make a donation to the PFA's benevolent fund in my case instead of paying a chunk to some agent. It's amicable, the club are happy and I'm greatly relieved. At last I'm getting good money to play a game I love and for a club I love. But I'm not rich overnight, as everyone assumes.

NOVEMBER 06

MARCUS HAHNEMANN'S PREMIERSHIP DIARY

DECEMBER

06

Downing some Red Bull at Newcastle.

December 1

I guess not many players can say going to Rochdale was the making of them, but it was for me. I look out for their results even now because the month I spent at Spotland in October 2001 restored my faith in the game and gave me the belief that what I was doing for a living really mattered.

Former Stoke midfielder and Mansfield boss Steve Parkin was the manager and he asked Fulham if he could have me for a month and off I went, not even knowing where the town was. At this time I was number three at Fulham and all I had to look forward to were reserve team games in front of a handful of people. I was not even on the first team bench and I badly needed at this stage of my development to find out what it was like to be a number one. Rochdale were struggling in Division Three, as they seem to do every year, but I had the time of my life. I really loved it. I was Rochdale's first ever American and the fans soon struck up a USA chant to make me feel at home, and I was right away.

I went from playing in fixtures where no-one noticed the result to playing in front of 3,000 people who cared deeply about the outcome of every match. It wasn't just the fans. The players gave everything all of the time. I was massively busy. I must have touched the ball a million times in the five league and two LDV games I played. I was involved from the first hectic minute to the last and had a fantastic time.

I trained one day a week at Fulham, but spent the rest of the time in the north and it was an education. I had a great month and at the end of it they wanted me for another. Trouble was, they couldn't afford the wages, so I never did go back. That was a shame. I fancied another few weeks there because I had discovered the proper meaning of football in this country. It's easy to support Manchester United, not so easy to be disappointed as they often are at clubs like Rochdale. But they are as passionate about their club as any Manchester United fan is about theirs.

I keep my affection for them half a dozen years down the line and subsequently I've met guys like Gareth Griffiths and Richard Jobson, who were Rochdale team-mates, at PFA meetings and they told me how much they appreciated me - a Premier League player - stepping down to play alongside them. I can only say the privilege was mine. They whetted my appetite for regular football and returning to Fulham was a real anti-climax.

December 2

Bolton is not a million miles from Rochdale, but in terms of team, stadium and expectation it might as well be at the other end of the earth. Today we are at home to Bolton and in our current mood we feel we can beat them. That's not to underestimate Bolton, far from it. Sam Allardyce always puts out a physically strong side and Steve Coppell has warned us that they're as competitive as ever. Not many managers would select a side in the way Allardyce does, but they always battle for everything and they play well together.

We edge it 1-0 thanks to another goal from Kevin Doyle. From my point of view it's another clean sheet, another solid defensive performance and a nice win bonus. I'm relieved.

December 5

Trips like tomorrow's to Newcastle used to be something of a nightmare for southern clubs like ours in terms of travelling, but as a sign of a step up in status we are flying up on the day and back

At the Bolton game, Jussi Jaaskelainen came up for a corner in search of an equaliser. It's a ploy I've used in the past.
so far without success.

again, so that we can be in our own beds not so many hours after the final whistle. Beds have been a problem for me in the past. Now on away trips I get a room to myself, but that wasn't always the case. I used to share a room with Murts (which I believe he may have told you about) and sometimes it's nice to have someone to chat to. But at one hotel, the beds were tiny. I'm 6ft 3 inches and my feet were hanging out of the bottom. I didn't sleep at all and that's no way to approach a match. Very often we would travel six hours by coach, arrive tired and then not be able to sleep. This time it felt like a cot and I went to our coach Kevin Dillon and said, "This is ridiculous". He agreed and I have been on my own ever since with the added comfort of a double bed.

Picking ideal room-mates is never straightforward. I go to bed after midnight, but James Harper, for instance, likes to be asleep on the eve of a match by 10.30pm. You have to have room-mates who are compatible, but it's not something I have to worry about now. I get a good night's sleep.

December 6

The plane journey to Newcastle is not smooth and nor is our performance. We lose 3-2 after being 2-1 ahead and after the way we have been playing, we have reason to be disappointed. Newcastle have been struggling and the crowd getting impatient with their players, so we felt we could draw at least. We would have been happy with that. James Harper scores both our goals, but with the game in our control, we went wrong.

From my perspective, there are a couple of things for me to think about on the way home. Newcastle get a penalty and I'm sure I would have saved it, but having guessed the right direction, the turf gave way as I dived and I slipped just as I got a hand to the ball. Obafemi Martins' shot goes in and there's nothing more I can do. Had I been able to get a tiny bit more traction, I'm sure I would have completed the save. Had that been at home, say, I'm positive I would have come out on top. The other is a shot from Emre which dips on its way past me into the net. I have to say it was a great strike, but I don't like conceding any type of goal and in the end I figure I was off my line one foot too far.

December 7

I admire James Harper. James is super fit, just about the fittest player at the club. He gets through a tremendous amount of work and not all of it is recognised. He's also a great passer of the ball and that comes from his personal regime. James is out on the training ground at 10am, well before the rest of us, practising his skills, working at the sort of things which make him so good. James is important to us and I think a little underrated. The talk is of Steve Sidwell being our midfield general, but Harper is a super player in his own right.

    Another aspect to him is how much of a team player he is, both in how he plays the game and his approach to his team-mates. Last night he had a cracking game, scoring twice, but on the plane on the way home he stood up and apologised to us all because he had lost the ball attempting something he feels now he shouldn't have in our own half which resulted in putting our defence under pressure and the penalty given away. That brought Newcastle back into the game at 2-2 and James went up even further in my, and I think everyone's, estimation.

December 9

Whenever we play Watford it always seems to be a 0-0 draw and, sure enough, so is this one. It's a high-pressure game for us. We are kind of natural rivals and we don't want to lose to them. But while we are having a good season, they are bottom already and it's not looking good for them. Dave at Costco, where we do our shopping, is looking forward to this. He's the Watford fan and reckons at Vicarage Road they will beat us, as he would.

    Brynjar Gunnarsson lives in Watford, having also played for the club, and knows how much they want to turn us over. I must have taken about 50 goal kicks and Watford make it difficult for us, as we knew they would. We are solid defensively and we need to be because Watford are in our faces from the start, never giving us an inch.

Not being far from Reading, we take plenty of fans with us and there is no way we are going to let them down. It's a rare game in that we are expected to win, but I guess most of us players are happy with the draw. The big thing was not to lose and Watford are definitely more disappointed by the result. Like every other club in the Premiership, they probably thought they would beat us at home.

December 10

Bobby Convey is having a difficult time with his knee injury. I feel sorry for him, not being in the team and there's talk of him going back to the United States for surgery. When I first came over I had my wife and kids for company and support. Bobby's pretty much on his own. I know something of what he's going through.

You gauge your self-worth by how you play. When you don't play, you wonder what you are supposed to be doing. There was a time at Fulham when I was continually on the bench. I was working hard in training all week and then being demoralised when the team sheet went up and I was not on it. My mother-in-law must have noted my mood one time and asked me how I felt. She sort of turned the question round so that I was answering it and the conclusion was that I was feeling sorry for myself. I sounded like a baby. Suddenly I came to my senses and realised how lucky I was. Life was not so bad. At that stage I don't think I was ready to be number one, so there I was playing tons of golf, living abroad, making more money than I ever did in the MLS and learning the game. I had to get over the fact that Fulham saw me as second best.

Bobby's been in and out of the team and I guess he's a bit dispirited sometimes, but he's more used to living in Britain now and once or twice I have been able to help him as a fellow American. He's got a lot more to give Reading.

Bobby Convey at our house for Christmas. Amanda's mom
brought him his favourite American Macaroni Cheese
as a joke Christmas present.

December 11

While Steve Coppell pulls the strings, his number two Kevin
Dillon runs training and has this habit of winding us all up behind
his smile. Kevin is a real wind-up merchant, but, like Wally
Downes, he has an important part to play within the management
structure at Reading and the three of them work together well,
each bringing different qualities to the job. As for Dill, we keep
thinking of ways to get our own back.

December 15

Our next two matches against Blackburn tomorrow and Everton the
following Saturday mean we will be up against two American
goalkeepers. Brad Friedel is a permanent fixture in the Blackburn

goal and Tim Howard is doing well during his season's loan at Everton from Manchester United. There are more Americans coming into the English game every season, many of them goalkeepers, and they are high quality players. It says something about the standard of players we are producing back in the States, and there are also an increasing number of outfield players, so that it's not unusual any more to find an American among the opposition.

December 16

I have been dreading this, the day I'm made to look just a little like a novice by one of these swerving footballs I've come to fear. Shots don't move in straight lines any more. They dip, twist, bend, anything but go straight. David Bentley beats me with a shot from long distance that moves all over the place like it has a mind of its own. At this level, the way these guys can send a ball spinning like a top, you can never know with any confidence where the hell it's going. This shot of Bentley's comes from nowhere and I thought at first it was heading for the top corner. But then it seemed to change direction as if destined for the middle of the goal and as I attempted to adjust, it went another way, dipping under the bar. I'm sure it looked a great goal on television, but these are nightmare moments for a goalkeeper. These shots can make you look stupid.

It's not a good day for any of us. We lose 2-1 at home to a middle ranking team, even after leading with a goal from James Harper. Some time ago we would not expect to beat Blackburn or Everton, but now we do and we should have won this one. It's a mark of how we have progressed. On paper we could never match up to most teams, but we have been finding ways to win, until today.

December 17

There's one less American in English football with Claudio Reyna's decision to go home. Claudio played his last game yesterday for Manchester City. Claudio is no youngster, but he's going back to play for the Red Bull in New York next week. He's had a great time over here with Rangers, Sunderland and Manchester City. The game in America needs guys with his sort of experience, putting something back.

Only Claudio knows if it's the right time to go home. Do you return to the States while you have a few years left? Or stay here where the money is and where the competition is fiercer?

James Harper slides home at Blackburn to make it three goals in as many games for the hard-working midfielder.

Not an easy decision. I played against Claudio for Reading in a pre-season friendly and he ran the show. I guess for him it's the right time to go, but so much depends on money and opportunities. Sure, our family miss things about America and we had a great time in Denver, but we still love living here and there are no thoughts of following Claudio home.

December 23

Steve Coppell is a self-contained man, not given to going mad if we lose or wildly celebrating if we win. But after we lose 2-0 at home to Everton today he hammers us.

We deserve it. Everton are a tough, hard-working team, they break up the play and wear us down. We have been super solid in defence, but somewhere along the line we lost a little of our focus today and we are punished. Even so, we cannot believe we have lost 2-0.

I'm an admirer of Andy Johnson, the Everton and England striker. He's in your face the whole time and makes some fantastic runs, but, being at home, I think we fancied our chances. There's a fine line between us playing well and the opposition playing badly, but this has not been a good week. We've played

Despite this save we still take a hammering from Everton and an ear-bashing from the manager.

Blackburn and Everton in seven days, both at home, and got nothing to show for it. As we come back into the dressing room, the manager is visibly upset and lets us have it with both barrels. "I will always back you up," he said. "But the mistakes you made are not acceptable. I'm disassociating myself from you guys today." There was silence, no dissenting voices. We had let him down and we knew it. More results like the last two and we are in for a very tough second half of the season.

December 24

Christmas Eve. Christmas is not a great time for footballers. Amanda knows football is my job, so it must come first and the kids have got used to me being away. When other families are gathered round the tree unwrapping presents or what ever, I'm packing my bags to go training or to head somewhere for an away match. "Ok boys, I'm going," I say. "Ok Dad, see you later," they say, not budging from their new toys. They've grown up with me not being there. I find that hard, but I console myself that it's not for ever.

Even at home there were always American Football games at Christmas, so it's been part of our lives for a long time. We'll train on Christmas evening before heading for a hotel in London prior to facing Chelsea for our Boxing Day game, so today we must celebrate. We have our turkey after training and we're nice and relaxed as families should be this time of year, only for us it's a day early.

December 25

We have five matches in a couple of weeks, so this is a hectic time. We have to be at the stadium to train under lights at 5.30pm. I say my farewells and there's nothing on the roads as I drive past houses lit up by tree lights, but I'm a happy man. I have with me a whole heap of turkey sandwiches. I reckon cold turkey sandwiches are just about the best part of Christmas food and for some reason I missed out on them at Thanksgiving. I don't know what happened to it (maybe the 32 guests had something to do with it), so I've made sure I've got plenty this time. We go through our final routines and then board the team bus for central London. We have a morning kick-off and it's sure to be a big match. But at least I have my turkey sandwiches with me in my bag.

December 26

The press make a big thing about our visit to Chelsea being a sort of grudge match, us against the angry Jose Mourinho, after the Stephen Hunt incident and all that. Not that Steve Coppell said anything about the composition of our team beforehand, but I don't think Stephen was ever going to play here. It would have placed him under incredible pressure and got the Chelsea fans wound-up.

I had no idea what sort of reception to expect once we got to Stamford Bridge, but no-one said anything about the previous time we played them, at least not to me. There's no tension or anything like that. I guess Chelsea have moved on as well.

Later......

We draw 2-2, which is one of our best results so far. Strangely, it's not our best performance. Spread over a season, this is a bad result for Chelsea, so they must be pleased to see the back of us. They discovered, as others have discovered, that we are not scared of anybody. We've been outclassed sometimes, but never really outworked, not while there's guys like Harper covering every blade and Shorey making those runs down the left. I still think he's too fat, though!

Every member of our team wants to get forward and score goals, which says something for our mentality, but today is like a lower league cup match, big against small, £3 million Reading against £150 million Chelsea. We play exactly the same way as we always do and always did last season when we won the Championship. During that year we never let our standards drop and the way we beat Middlesbrough on the opening day of this season showed nothing had changed.

We played the way we normally do, but we did make one concession to the fact we were playing the champions. Kevin Doyle dropped into midfield because we felt Geremi would see a lot of the ball and there's no doubt Chelsea are not always able to find their rhythm. I'm annoyed when Didier Drogba gets a goal against me. I was clearly held down by him, so that I was not able to jump as we compete, but the referee was happy with it. It sucked. He's a strong guy, Drogba, and he was all over me, somehow scoring, I think, between my arm and a leg.

December 27

Leroy Lita scored one of our goals at Chelsea and I'm really impressed by the improvement he's making all the time. He's great at holding up the ball and his timing in the air from my distribution is tremendous. Being so much faster than most people, he was being caught offside in the Championship even

Drogba scores for Chelsea in the 2-2 draw.

when he wasn't, so timing his runs is vital. Thierry Henry is a fantastic example of a guy who does the right things at the right time, but Lits is getting there. He unsettles defences even at this level with his pace and he's learning all the time. I think he could become a big asset in time even if he hasn't played much so far this season.

December 29

No sooner have we got over the Chelsea experience than we head tomorrow for Old Trafford. Life doesn't get any easier!

Yet it's not fear I'm experiencing right now, but excitement at the prospect of playing in front of 75,000 people in such a super stadium. This is why I've

Leroy Lita celebrates his goal against Chelsea with Sonko, who was to get on the scoresheet in the next match at Old Trafford.

dedicated my life to being a professional footballer, so that I might perform at places like this. It's going to be a proud moment, made all the better because Amanda and the boys will be there to sample the incredible atmosphere. I'm so pleased about that.

All the guys are really looking forward to this. Glen Little's actually a Manchester United fan and this will be a big day for him, but there's no split loyalties. He'll give everything for us as he always does.

December 30

I've never been to Old Trafford before and it lives up to expectations. We lose 3-2, but in truth they are more comfortable than that. Sonko keeps us in it. He's a great header of the ball and is just outstanding. He also scores one of our goals with a typical header. As at Chelsea, we showed we were not going to be intimidated, but there's not much you can do about guys like Ronaldo. He's ridiculously good. We couldn't get the ball off him. Forget about all those step-overs, he has so many other attributes. He's great in the air and brave.

We aren't helped by Sam Sodje being sent off in a bizarre incident. Sam held back Wayne Rooney, but only after offside had already been given. It was probably a yellow card, but not a red one and it's the last thing you need, down to ten men at Old Trafford. Very frustrating.

I'm not one of those people who think Manchester United get more than their share of big decisions in their favour. At home, and often away, they have 80 per cent of the possession. They get the ball and run at you, again and again, so that sooner or later you are going to concede free kicks and penalties.

From my individual point of view, it wasn't such a bad game. I made three or four saves, Ryan Giggs tried to chip me and I am also claiming an assist for Lita's goal. I launched the ball down field, Shane Long and a defender missed it and Lita ran on to score. But then again, I might even have scored a goal myself. How good would that have been? Right at the end I went up for a corner and suddenly found myself clear at the near post in a huge gap. All Shorey had to do was hit it to me, but instead he aimed it to the far post and my moment of possible glory was gone forever. I once had a header cleared off the line at Norwich, but this would have topped the lot. Still, it's a great day despite defeat.

December 31

End of year and time for reflection. I reckon the Premiership is broken up into four tiers with United, Chelsea, Liverpool and Arsenal in tier one. We would have expected to lose all eight of those games, so that anything other than defeat is a bonus: and we've already got two points from them. We've still got Arsenal away and Liverpool at home, but so far we have taken a point off Manchester United and another from Chelsea, so we have done better than we dared hope. Of course there are plenty of other top class sides, but we have to be happy with what we have achieved so far. We've got 27 points as we enter 2007 and that's great. We should get enough from the remainder of the season to be able to forget about relegation.

Steve Coppell prevents us getting ahead of ourselves. His commonsense and meticulous approach won't allow us to think we have completed the job. There's a long way to go. He knows it and so do we.

One on One with Ronaldo.

Two very different kinds of relaxation I enjoy.
(Above) On a fishing trip with Hunter and Austin on the
Yakima river near Seattle.
...and (Below) speeding round the track on an advanced driving
course. Man, I love anything on four wheels!

MARCUS HAHNEMANN'S PREMIERSHIP DIARY

JANAURY

07

Sylvester Stallone at Goodison Park.

January 1

Amanda writes...

Our major fund-raising events are coming up in the New Year, but today we are spending the first morning of 2007 in a car park. Steve McDonald, the manager at Costco next to the Madejski Stadium, and Debbie Robinson are letting us have the use of their car park. BBC Radio Berkshire have done us proud by broadcasting the event live. My boys find an inflatable goal for kids to shoot into. No sign of Marcus, but then he has got a game this afternoon. Costco donate 300 mince pies and at the end of a good morning our charities are going to be £2,700 better off.

Amanda's mom being interviewed on BBC local radio live at the Costco car park Royals Families event.

Marcus writes...

I have known West Ham keeper Robert Green a long time. I played against him when he was at Norwich, so he's been around a year or two. Not so long ago in Chicago, when he was playing for England and I was among the American subs, we traded shirts.

Some of my shirts are in America, others in England, but I prize them all. I think the one I regard as special is the shirt I wore for my 200th start for Reading against Arsenal. My dad has that one. To play 200 games for one club these days in England has to be special because players move around so much and it will always mean a lot to me.

The reason I mention Green is that he's on the end of a mighty beating today when West Ham lose to us 6-0. We needed a win. We'd only picked up two points from our previous six matches, so our confidence was just a little down. Alan Curbishley had always done a decent job at Charlton and had made a good start at West Ham by beating Manchester United in his first game, but today it goes wrong for him and his team. It's kind of weird because for the first ten or 15 minutes, the match is pretty even and tight and looks like developing into a really good contest. I make one early save that pleases me and at that stage West Ham are playing some nice stuff. But from the moment we our score first goal, they collapse. We could have got ten, no exaggeration, and if had not been for Green they would have been even more humiliated. That's the thing about being a goalie. You can have a blinding match and still concede six goals.

Okay, we were up for the game and never held back even when it was clear we were going to win. But the way West Ham folded was incredible. Shorey set up four of the goals and his

**Anton Ferdinand heads into his own goal
for the third against West Ham.**

crosses at set plays were absolutely ridiculously good. When he plays like this, have England got anyone better?

I go to commiserate with Green at the final whistle. No goalkeeper deserves that to happen to him. Green made three good saves that I can remember, but I decide to keep the consolation to a minimum. "What the f*** happened there?" I said to him as we shake hands. I didn't expect a reply.

January 3

Green's capable, but for me no-one touches Edwin van der Sar. I rate Edwin as the best goalkeeper in the league, as good as any I have ever seen. I know people say Petr

Alan Curbishley had felt the pressure at Charlton, where he was one of the longest serving managers in the Premiership, but the result on New Year's Day showed he had jumped from the frying pan into the fire.

Cech is number one and, yes, he runs him close, but it's Edwin every time for me. When Fulham signed Edwin I was pushed down the order at Craven Cottage to number three behind him and Maik Taylor. I could say with some justification he drove me out, but I prefer the positive option. I thank him for giving me a chance. There was no way Fulham could keep the three of us happy and I was getting to the stage where I needed regular football, so I had to look around for another club. No way was I going home to America until I found out if I was good enough to do that. The signing of van der Sar led eventually to me joining Reading and for that I will always be grateful.

What I like about Edwin is his superb footwork, his distribution and the way he comes - and gets - crosses. There are plenty of other great keepers around. Shay Given is fantastic and has been great for so long, Brad Friedel also, but he hates Tool, so nobody's perfect. Tim Howard likes R&B which is hard to understand. For sheer athletic ability, though, there's no-one to touch David James. I first came across him at Aston Villa and was astounded by the way he came for crosses I would not even consider coming for. For his age, he's a top player and an inspiration to people like me who are younger and worried when it all might end. Kasey Keller's a buddy. I keep in touch with him. We're from the same part of the US, so we have that in common, but we have known each other a long time - and he likes Tool.

Who's the second best keeper in the Premier League? I try to say this without arrogance, but I believe it to be me. I have to believe it and all the other keepers will back themselves in the same way.

January 4

We get the papers every day at the training ground and we, the players, are always amazed at the discrepancies in reports and in the marks out of ten the reporters allocate us. You wonder what they are watching sometimes. I have gone from an average six to a star man nine all in the same match, depending on which paper you read. The papers do affect things, no doubt, and the marks are talking points among us. I know how good or bad I have been in a match, so I don't need telling, and in any case goalkeeping coach Sal Bibbo is there to talk me through the game I've just played.

I know some players get quite down about their marks from people not always qualified to give them, but I shrug it off. What surprises me more is what reporters consider to be important. 'Beaten on his near post' is an expression they often use. Is that any more of a crime than being beaten at the far post? We have to try to cover the whole goal. Does it count for two goals if it goes in at the near post?

January 5

Steve Coppell is continuing his policy of giving as many squad members as possible a game in the cup matches. Graham Stack took my place in the Carling Cup and Adam Federici will stand in for the FA Cup third round match at home to Burnley. Stacky is now on loan at Leeds and it's a big step for Adam, who, when he's not playing on his Italian parentage, is telling us he's Australian. Not that I know much about cricket, but he's enjoying the Ashes series. He reminds as many of the English guys as possible about how their team is being hammered in Australia on a daily basis and there's not much response.

January 9

I've been on the bench before, but not for home games and it's strange being a substitute at the Madejski today. I'm not sure what to do. I'm off the pitch, but not off it, if you see what I mean, and I have to be ready to go on at a moment's notice. Adam's a good young player and he makes some important saves as Burnley come back from 3-0 down to 3-2. When we score, I go nuts, more than I would have done if I'd been playing. I admit that's hard to explain. At half-time, Sal asks me if I want anything, meaning some shots to get me warmed up. "A hot dog," I tell him.

Amanda writes...

Our launch and champagne-tasting in November produced an unexpected bonus. Russell Kempson, a sports writer with *The Times* and a veteran Reading-watcher, noted what the Royals Families were attempting to achieve and wrote a nice article on us for his paper. That in itself was good, but the feature was spotted by Margaret Haines in the office of the Lieutenancy of Berkshire, who alerted Sophie, the Countess of Wessex. She was only too keen to visit the Madejski Stadium for a coffee morning to help give our organisation a little support, publicity and impetus. Being royalty, everybody had to be vetted and all entrances checked.

But despite all that, the Countess was very down-to-earth and was genuinely fascinated by our fund-raising and endorsed our choices of charity. She met our committee and Karen and I said a few words of welcome. Then we introduced her to representatives of PACT and Berkshire Women's Aid. Later she also met some of our Gold Sponsors, among them Kyocera, Haslams, Wicom Group, the Reading Evening Post, Costco, Sue Roberts and the Broad Street Mall group. The Countess had extensive experience in her own public relations company so she was able to offer us little bits of advice. We have to be pleased

The Royals Families girls at the Madejski.

with getting some enthusiastic royal backing and the excellent coverage in the Reading Evening Post further raised awareness of what we are trying to do within the community. The Royal Families are up and running.

January 14

I made an error which costs us a goal and two points at Everton today. All of that in front of the man who plays Rocky and Rambo, my boyhood heroes; one of most people's heroes, I guess. Sylvester Stallone, who made both characters international film icons, is in England promoting his latest *Rocky* picture. It so happens he's a guest of Everton and is watching us. Federici is all pumped up in the dressing room before the match, doing a spot of shadow boxing. By chance Steve Sidwell has the Rocky theme, *Eye of the Tiger* on his iPod and he shares it with us. We never did get to meet Stallone, but he rose to acknowledge the applause from the crowd when he took his seat in the directors' box, so I was aware of him and where he was.

I can't blame him, or his dodgy keeping in the film *Escape To Victory*, for the goal, though. We felt we owed Everton one. At our place we had let them dominate and we were determined not to let that happen again. Steve Coppell says we must not let Everton bully us and collectively we play well and get a 1-1 draw. But Andy Johnson's goal will haunt me for days, maybe weeks. In short, I make an error of judgement. Johnson is an aggressive, tenacious player and when a cross comes over I think I can get there before him. But I don't. Johnson is so quick, he's there half a second before me and heads the ball into the net, leaving me stranded yards off my line. I know I've blundered. I just don't make mistakes like that normally, so it's hard to take. It never occurred to me Johnson would literally beat me to my punch. At the final whistle I'm inconsolable and this time even Sal cannot find an excuse for my error of judgement. He says I shouldn't have left my line and of course he's right. On the long journey home I have a lot of time to think about it. Later the gaffer spots me brooding. "Don't beat yourself up over it," he says and I feel better for that, but at the moment, not much. I feel I've let the team down.

My mistake at Goodison Park lets in Andy Johnson and Everton.

January 15

I'm still angry about that goal. We play Sheffield United at home on Saturday and I'm anxious to get out there and get the mistake out of my system. I broke one of the fundamental rules of goalkeeping. If you decide to come for a cross, you must get it. It's a bad error, but being with the family puts it in perspective and allows it to drift out of my thoughts occasionally.

January 16

Goalkeeping is an art, it requires a lot of work to perfect it and it doesn't get any easier. Any goal that goes in against me, I think about my part in it. Was I in the wrong position? Could I have anticipated quicker? That sort of thing. The worst mistake I ever made was on my debut for Fulham against Sheffield Wednesday. There was a corner, the ball came to a defender on the near post chest high and somehow it got through him. I ended up punching the ball into the corner of the net. I say to myself 'the defender missed the header', but it couldn't have done my chances of becoming number one at Fulham any good.

So far this season I think I should have saved the free-kick which led to a Middlesbrough goal on the opening day, that Bentley shot for Blackburn gives me nightmares and I feel aggrieved by Drogba's goal at Stamford Bridge. He grabbed me and I should have grabbed him back, but you only have to make a tiny mistake in that respect and it's a penalty. Some of these guys go down very easily. I like watching *Match of the Day* on Saturday evenings when I'm properly relaxed, but they only ever show the goals, not the saves, at least not many saves. Maybe I'm watching it with goalkeeper's spectacles on.

January 17

I had to start all over again almost, learning about goalkeeping, when I came to England. While moving from the States was not a culture shock, as such, England took a bit of getting used to. What did I miss about home? Family and friends, naturally, a Starbucks on every corner, canned caffeine, the open spaces. To begin with I pined for sugared cereals like Lucky Charms and Captain Crunch and peanut butter. Being American we like our coffee and we used to have to get the beans from any Starbucks we could find. But it's all changed gradually. Starbucks (a Seattle company) rule the world, Red Bull satisfies my caffeine thirst and Costco supply all the cereals we once had to ask relatives to bring over for us. Marmite? How can you guys eat that stuff? But in the end, it is the big open spaces which we took for granted back in the States that Amanda and I crave. A year or two back we looked at a three-acre piece of land an hour from Seattle for sale at about £100,000. I guess it would be hard to find anything similar in England.

Amanda writes...

Actually it was a Starbucks in Wimbledon, where we lived when we first came to England, in which we met some Americans who became instant best friends. The husband was working as a banker and now the family have gone back to the States where they have four children. I felt a bit guilty about coming all the way to London and becoming friends with some Americans straight away, but it wasn't easy coming to terms with living abroad.

Fulham actually showed us accommodation in Barnes before we chose Wimbledon. There's a big American community in Wimbledon and when we heard a loudspeaker a couple of blocks away we realised we were close to the tennis championships. Later we sampled the centre court, strawberries and cream, and loved it, but while Marcus went off training and found friends that way, I was not working, was not driving and was stuck with a baby.

There was a shock or two, being a new country and a huge city. I remember how we used to leave the internet on at home all day, as we did in Colorado, and got a bill for £300. Local calls were free in the States and so we didn't add to our phone bill by dialling up. Fulham got me a Renault, so that I was able to get out and about. I never saw myself as a stay-at-home mum in any case. Soon we built up a circle of friends from somewhere other than America. Even so, another American, footballer Eddie Lewis and his wife Mari, were close, Marcus's colleague Steve Finnan lived in Wimbledon and we were soon mixing socially with the families of Maik Taylor and the van der Sars.

I went to all home games and many away, even though Marcus was usually only a substitute, and we quickly settled. We had taken a pay cut, when you added Marcus's salary from the Rapids to mine, so we had made many sacrifices to come to England to see if he could cut it in what we believed to be the best league in the world. We were here for the long haul and not inclined to go home until we found out - one way or another - if Marcus was good enough to be a number one. I knew he was and even in the darkest days at Fulham when it looked as if he might never get a game of any sort, his attitude was superb.

January 19

Sheffield United, again. Tomorrow we face our old rivals at the Madejski Stadium, looking to complete the double over them, having beaten them up there in September. What is it about Neil Warnock? He always has something interesting to say, a bit like Mourinho, but it seems you either hate him or like him. He has this capacity to wind-up the opposition and their fans, though I think in his way he's good for the game. Last season we were numbers one and two all season in the Championship, so the rivalry between the clubs is intense. As I've said before, I like their guys. They are all tough competitors and probably mirror their gaffer.

January 20

We beat Sheffield United 3-1, but the result is only the half of the story. Hunty is elbowed by Keith Gillespie and a few players get involved in some minor scuffling, while Gillespie, who had only just come on, is shown the red card. But the trouble gets worse when Neil Warnock apparently gestures to his own players to break the legs of one of ours. Wally Downes reacts furiously. Wally was only trying to protect us and he's a good man to have in your corner. I'm stuck in my goal watching all this. So is Paddy Kenny, the Sheffield United goalkeeper. I catch his eye at the other end of the pitch and put up my fists to offer him a mock fight. He laughs. It's amazing what you see from your goal.

January 22

There's some bad news about Ibrahima Sonko. He's damaged cruciate knee ligaments and that means six months out of the

Keith Gillespie receives his marching orders.

Above and below: Round One and Round Two of the fracas between us and Sheffield United.

game and, of course, an operation. I'm going to miss him because he's a dominant defender and not easily replaced. Steve Coppell wants to keep the extent of the injury quiet in case other clubs try to hike up the prices when he tries to sign a replacement from them. Sonks has been a huge success this season, bridging the gap between the Premier League and the Championship with ease. The best he can hope for at this stage is to be fit for the start of next season and in the meantime, until we get someone in, we must try to cover the gap. The transfer window closes at the end of the month so the gaffer doesn't have much time.

January 23

Ulysses de la Cruz scored a great goal against Sheffield and we're pleased for him. 'El Presidente' is a quiet sort of guy and because of the language barrier, communication with him isn't easy. As a result I don't think we've discovered his true personality yet, but he's popular. Dela sends back some of his wages to his home village in Ecuador, never forgetting the family and friends he left behind in some poverty. He's also unbelievably strong, built like a bull. You can only marvel when he gets on the weights and he's proving to be a good signing because whenever he comes into the team in midfield or at right-back he does well.

January 25

Steve Coppell has made another of his swoops on the League of Ireland to sign Alan Bennett, a 24 year-old Republic of Ireland international. He's already had one game in the reserve team and he certainly looks as if he could be one for the future. He's not a youngster at all, but if he can be as successful as Kevin Doyle and adapt in the same way he could make a big impact as there's a place up for grabs in front of me now Sonks is out of action.

January 27

Our victory over Burnley in the third round of the FA Cup means we must travel to Birmingham for the fourth. They're up among the clubs at the top of the Championship looking to follow us into the Premiership. Steve Coppell is mindful that there's still a long way to go in the league and will stick with his policy of resting players like me. Fans want him to pick our best team, but Steve is going to give another chance to Adam Federici, Sam Sodje, Seol Ki-Hyeon and John Oster. Bikey's going to take Sonks' place in the centre of defence and Bobby Convey's going to get a game. Me? I'm on the bench.

January 28

Facing Birmingham gives me the chance to catch up with Maik Taylor. He was number one at Fulham and I was number two, but the rivalry meant nothing. It was only professional because we always got on well. Like me Maik has German roots. He was born there, but has played a whole heap of games for Northern Ireland due to his parents' nationality. I think I learned something from him at Fulham and in many ways it was he who lost most when Edwin van der Sar pitched up. Sure, I was surplus to requirements all of a sudden, but looked around and eventually got another club. Maik had been first choice for years until van der Sar came along and it couldn't have been easy finding a club of similar stature.

Maik was in the army until he was in his early 20s and came to English football late, like me I guess, so we have that in common. He has three boys, a young family like ours, and it's clear that he still has an appetite for the game and a desire to keep up his standards. We talked of everything except football, at least not about this match, and I know he badly wants another crack at the Premiership at 35. Good luck to him, I hope Birmingham go up for his sake. I remember Paul Bracewell, the Fulham manager at the time, telling me when I joined the club that he wanted me to push Taylor, but he's such a good goalkeeper, it was never going to be that straightforward.

Later....

We beat Birmingham 3-2. Lita gets two of the goals and looks in sharp form. It'll be interesting to see if the manager goes back on his fringe-player policy now that we're through to the fifth round, the last 16. My guess is he won't.

January 29

Two or three days ago we signed another goalkeeper, Mikkel Andersen from Copenhagen. He's a big guy for 18 and is one for the future, but it's a reminder that nothing stands still for long. We have seven keepers. Stacky's still at Leeds, but Federici has done superbly in the FA Cup games, taking his chance well. To be honest I had not seen much of him in a competitive environment, but he's improved a lot and pushing me hard. Ben Hamer's gaining experience at Conference club Crawley and we have a couple coming through at under-18 level. Now Andersen is with us. He will need time to mature and learn his trade, as we all had to do.

January 30

We beat Wigan 3-2 today, but I'm not happy with Wigan's first goal. Emile Heskey hit it hard and early from distance and it swerved a lot on its way inside my near post. You just don't get shots come at you like that in the Championship. At this level you have to expect the unexpected. I think it was saveable and coming at 0-0, it's a shock to the system. Luckily it wakes us up and the team responds positively to the challenge. We have always somehow found ways to get back into games and that's what we do again. I'm not surprised to see Ivar Ingimarsson among the goals. He likes to get forward and it's a boost for defenders to score. Normally their reward is a clean sheet, but Ivar deserved his goal, out-jumping a defender.

January 31

The transfer window closes today. Steve Coppell has been busy, as we figured he might be. Bikey has joined us permanently from Moscow, Michael Duberry of Stoke will be seen as our replacement for Sonks and Greg Halford becomes our record signing when we pay Colchester £2 million for him. I hear he's a long throw specialist, which might add to our weaponry, but he'll need time to come to terms with the Premiership, as we all did. Alan Bennett has followed Kevin Doyle and Shane Long from Cork and if he proves half as good, there will be no complaints from us. I reckon some of our fans thought we might be bringing in a big name or two, but that's not the way the manager works. Sure, we needed cover for Sonks as an immediate remedy, but we know about Bikey and the others are for the future. This is the way Reading do business...

...I'm amazed the transfer deadline has come and gone and we haven't lost a single player. There was talk of Sidwell inevitably, but no-one came in for him, so he's with us until the end of the season when his contract expires. Then we lose him for nothing, although I know Reading are doing all they can to find enough money to keep him. Sidwell's been great for us all season and he's not playing like a man about to move on. If he has a deal lined up at the end of the season, he's concealing it well. None of us know where he's going, he won't let on. No question he'll be missed, but there's a few months left of the season so perhaps we can persuade him to stick with us. I'll work on him. Better to be a regular with us than a reserve at a bigger club, but, as I say, I think Steve is not going anywhere cheaply in terms of wages...

...No, what annoys me about the transfer deadline's lack of activity as regards Reading is the implication that no other club thinks we, the players, are good enough. I was sure someone would put in a bid for Kevin Doyle, for instance, and there were rumours of one, but it hasn't developed. We are seventh in the Premier League, there have been some super individual performances within the team's rise up the ladder, but it's as if no-one has noticed. We read all the gossip in the papers and none

Steve Sidwell in action - a great season has led
to an inevitable departure this summer.

of us ever got a mention in the build up to the deadline. A lot of the guys are talking about it, the absence of any Reading players being wanted by the bigger clubs. In a way it's like it's an insult. I should stress no-one wants to leave Reading. We all enjoy being here and in a way it's nice not to be distracted. So none of this matters, but it's still a mystery. Anyway the deadline has come and gone and we've spent £3 million. We just don't dish out contracts in all directions, as some clubs appear to do.

Helping promote the Berkshire Fire Service along with Dave Kitson (left) and a young firewoman. I enjoy this kind of work and it's really important that everyone realises how vital the emergency services are.

FEBRUARY

07

My parents and the boys enjoy a great night out at Old Trafford for our FA Cup tie, while I watch from the bench.

February 1

This promises to be a big month for us. The draw for the fifth round of the FA Cup, made a few days ago, will take us to Old Trafford and the big talking point in the papers again is what sort of team we'll send up there. I was with Federici at the training ground when the draw was made and he could hardly believe it. He was on the phone to his Dad in Australia pretty much straight away. Dill felt we would get Watford away, while I thought we would be paired with Plymouth, again away. We were both wrong. Any home draw would have been great for us, but when Manchester United came out of the hat, it was a bit of a shock.

I still had some friends over from the States staying with us and they wondered if I would be playing. It's kind of hard explaining that, although I am first choice, I probably wouldn't be in the team. Why not? Well, our policy is to play squad players in the FA Cup. Steve Coppell could, with some justification, pick the team which is our best one, but I'm sure he won't change, even when our opponents are Manchester United, just about the biggest club in the world. Sure, having played at Old Trafford once this season, I would love to play again, but I'm not going to begrudge Federici the greatest moment of his career.

Steve is coming under a bit of pressure from fans, who fear a thrashing, and the Press who can't believe, as a former Manchester United player, he won't buckle and put out his best eleven. But the manager is not budging. He says it's an insult to guys like Oster, de la Cruz, Convey and Seol, who are, after all, internationals in their own right, to list them as reserves and in any case he sticks to his belief that no-one outside the top four big clubs is going to win the competition.

February 2

The FA Cup aside, the talking point is Europe. I find it unbelievable. Never in my life did I think I would be talking about the possibility of playing against the major teams in the UEFA Cup and even now I prefer not to dwell on it for long. Perhaps predictably, Steve Coppell's not talking about it, none of the players either, but on the other hand we never expected to have 37 points by the end of January. There are three places available for English clubs to compete in the UEFA Cup and it can't be ruled out that we might be one of them. I would have been happy with 37 points over the whole of a season, to be honest. Premier League safety's just a few points away, we might even have enough already, and if we carry on as we are, Europe may be there for the taking.

I think it's unrealistic, too much too soon. Our squad is not big enough to cope with the many extra games a run of success in the UEFA Cup would mean. Everyone remembers what happened to Ipswich when they got into Europe soon after promotion and crashed. We wouldn't want that to happen to us. There's a lot of teams ahead and behind us in the table at the moment, so I reckon it's unlikely we'll qualify, but who knows? So far, we've surprised everyone, including even ourselves, but our record indicates how difficult it can be. We have lost a league match 4-0 and won another 6-0. In the Championship, anybody can beat anybody on a given day. That's not the way things happen in the Premier League.

February 3

We travel to Manchester City today with 37 points and come home with three more after winning 2-0. We play super well, as we have done so often this season. To reach a landmark 40 points is just incredible. How the hell have we done it? Everyone's pretty happy on the coach home because, although no-one's saying it, we must be safe now. Safe with 12 games to go. Mission accomplished.

    The City of Manchester's a nice stadium and DaMarcus Beasley, an American, makes it extra interesting by being among the opposition. Lita gets both our goals with perfect timing from his point of view since the England Under-21 manager Stuart Pearce is also in charge of Manchester City. It's a huge deal for Lits. I've mentioned him more than once, but we have a really good relationship and spend a lot of time together. There is an arrogance about him, but I think he can go a long way in this game. I try to help him in shooting drills and he listens to my advice. If he has a fault it is that he tries to be too precise in his shooting, looking for the perfect goal. I tell him to get his shot on target, that's all that matters. His two goals are all the more creditable because he's a sub and Pearce could not have failed to notice him. The shooting at this level is still a shock to me. They shoot quicker, before you are set. In the Championship, as they prepare to shoot at you, there's enough time to get a water bottle out of the back of the net.

Celebrating victory at the City of Manchester stadium.

February 4

I didn't sleep well Saturday night. I'm still fired up, thinking about it all. I start to think ahead to next season, a little dangerous maybe, but there will be Premier League football at the Madejski Stadium barring total disaster and I never thought I would be saying that in the first week of February.

Then I don't sleep well Sunday night either. It's the Super Bowl and, while my team Seattle Seahawks are not in it this year as they were last, I stay up to watch. That leads me to think of people back home and I get on the phone to them and before long another night's gone and I'm not properly rested.

February 6

I couldn't get any proper sleep Monday either. I'm still pumped up, I guess, but on Tuesday morning I really struggle to wake up and that's most unlike me. The result is just about the worst training session of my life. Sal Bibbo watches balls bounce off me and asks me, "What's the matter?" I just can't get myself going. The harder I try the worse it gets. "Buddy, what's wrong?" Sal says finally. "I'm tired," I tell him. It's not much of an excuse, but it's true. I'm exhausted. Tonight I sleep soundly and feel a lot better for it.

February 7

We have a day off today. I get up a little later and get on my bike and go for a long ride and at last I'm returning to normal. Normally I love training: the harder it is, the more I like it. I volunteer for extra roll-backs and half-volleys to finish a session most days to get the feet moving, which is a vital part of a goalkeeper's game. Two hours physical hard work each day is right for me, so I can't be sure what happened earlier this week. Just a reaction of some kind and I'm over it now.

February 8

My mother-in-law in America points out on the internet that I have been named in the Actim Team of the Week, a selection based on facts like shots saved and blocked, distribution, clearances, passes, tackles, assists, that sort of thing. It's an achievement and I'm flattered. My own mother tells me: "I always said you were the best goalkeeper in the league and now you've proved it." Who am I to disagree with my mother? [There were three other Reading players in the team: Lita, Little and Ingimarsson.]

February 9

The United States are playing Mexico soon in their first international since the World Cup. Bob Bradley is the coach now, replacing Bruce Arena, and I'm not in his first squad. I don't know Bradley, although I played against him in the MLS. I'm a little disappointed. I don't want to think my involvement with the national team is over. Perhaps he's experimenting, perhaps

Leroy Lita in action against Villa, against whom he scored again following his brace against Man City.

my time is up. Only time will tell. I'm not picked, so there's nothing I can do about it. I guess it's another fixture in the middle of a week in an already crowded schedule, so from that point of view I'm not complaining. But I still do want to play for my country.

February 10

We beat Villa 2-0 at home today. That's nine clean sheets out of 27 and I make a couple of great saves, which I'm pleased with. One was a shot from distance. I took one step backwards as the ball came my way and at full stretch got a finger tip on it. The other was from their new striker John Carew, after a shot had rebounded to him off a post. I knew he would smash it at me because of the tightness of the angle and he did. Villa had a go at us, but we love to attack and there was plenty of scope to do

I save from Ashley Young.

that. Sometimes we leave ourselves open, but once every three Premier League matches we don't let in a goal, so we must be doing something right. Those critics who said we would slide down the table eventually have been answered. To be in the top half is incredible, but now we're sixth and that's so far-fetched. Sidwell gets both our goals. If he goes, he's going to be a big miss.

The talk in the papers is again of Reading in Europe. They've changed their tune. So far I've only been to Germany, Spain and Portugal, so I might get to see a bit more if we continue like this.

February 12

Steve Coppell has a dry wit, so it's rare to see him laugh out loud. But he did once. Stephen Hunt went to cross with his left foot in training, but hit the ball into touch with his trailing plant leg, his right. Sure, it was funny. He couldn't have done it again if he had tried. But none of us were ready for the gaffer's reaction. He laughed like a drain and surprised us all.

February 13

I'm in the Actim Team of the Week again and in terms of performances, I'm 19th best among all the players in any position in the league. This is something I could never have imagined and just part of a crazy time the whole team's having.

European qualification may not happen for us, but at least we are contenders. There are clubs out there in the Premier League with four times the pay packets and three times the crowd who will not be in Europe next season, whatever happens between now and the middle of May.

February 14

Today is the Valentine's Ball and I'm pissed off because it means I have to put on a suit. I don't like wearing a suit and while the ball doesn't start until 8pm, I'm told to be at the Madejski Stadium two hours earlier because Meridian TV are doing a live feed into their evening programme at about 6.30pm and they want to interview me. Karen Murty was there and, of course, Amanda because this is one of the big fund-raising events of the Royals Families' calendar. But then, just as I get ready to go on, Meridian decide to interview Karen and Graeme instead. So I'm here two hours early in a suit for nothing. Sucks.

Amanda writes...

We have to be pleased how well this went. We raised £21,000 from a three-course sit-down meal and auction. Glen Little was the auctioneer and very good he was too. In total we had some 300 or more guests and everybody had a good time, even Marcus, once he had got over his suit problem. One of the auction 'prizes' was the first dance of the evening with a shirt-less Ibrahima Sonko. The girls were queuing up for the chance and someone paid £700. Earlier Simon Cox, Doyle and Sonko help us gather another £1,100 selling roses in the Broad Street Mall. The players are joining enthusiastically in Royals Family occasions. Tonight we had Sonko, Murty, Convey, Harps and Sidwell among the guests. Marcus's parents enjoyed the night, too. There are three more big events to come this season and it's gone unbelievably well so far.

FEBRUARY 07

My mom and I at the Royals Families' Valentine's Ball.
I hated wearing that suit and tie!

February 15

There's talk of Arsenal forging a link with my old club, Colorado Rapids, and I'm all for it. English football is the most exciting in the world and it's very popular among American viewers and growing ever more so. I wish we at Reading could do something similar because there are some good young players coming through here who would benefit from playing for a spell in the MLS. It makes sense from a marketing point of view too and I reckon Arsenal and Colorado Rapids will profit from the idea. There are also some brilliant young guys in America who would improve if they came to a club like Arsenal, or, even better, Reading.

February 16

One of the drawbacks of links like those between Arsenal and Colorado Rapids is that more and more overseas players are coming to England. I'm in no position to condemn that because when I was in America there was only one league I wanted to watch on television and I did everything I could to get over here. Keller and Friedel were already here. English players are more expensive, so clubs tend to look abroad for value for money. I read how there's a drinking culture among English players, but that's not true in my view. Anyway, foreign players like a drink too. It doesn't touch me. I'm at a different stage of my life and I don't like nightclubs because of the music they play. Maybe it's because I came here late, but I don't take anything for granted.

February 17

Steve Coppell has stayed true to his word and our team is pretty much the same as in the third and fourth rounds when we go up to Old Trafford for the fifth. This means I'm on the bench and Adam Federici is in goal. This is the biggest match of his career by a long, long way and his Dad has come over from a small town in New

South Wales to watch his son. Adam has given up a lot to make it in England, sleeping on floors when he first arrived and learning his trade out on loan. We have a great relationship and if I can teach him anything, I will do. We have a lot of competition in training and even in the weights room, but I'm aware there are 70,000 people out there and this is only his third senior game. He's pumped up and I'm pumped up for him and the rest of the team.

I give him a little advice before he goes out into the arena, which is sure to take his breath away. He's nervous and wants to play well for the team and for his Dad, who's travelled 10,000 miles. I say to him, "Keep doing what you normally do. Do what you know you can." It's an odd thing about goalkeeping, sometimes deep down you want guys to shoot towards the top corner so you can leap across your goal and make a spectacular save, but the professional in you wants the forward to scuff it wide. I hope for Adam's sake he doesn't have to leap across his goal too often.

Later...

Adam makes an absolutely fantastic save to stop Henrik Larsson scoring the winner. Any keeper would have been proud of that and it will live with him for ever, and his Dad. All those people who said we'd be swamped have been proved wrong and we are good value for a 1-1 draw. Brynjar Gunnarsson gets our equaliser with a header from a corner and on the bench there's mayhem. Even the boss forces a smile at the final whistle. He deserves some praise for sticking to his beliefs. Now we have a replay to look forward to and I guess I'll be a substitute again, but Adam's done a fantastic job so far.

February 19

Sonko is having his operation later this week. The cruciate knee ligaments will be repaired and all he will be able to do is rest it and then begin the process of recovery. He's a totally different player from the one I first saw in an early game at Ipswich. Sonks was so nervous, he looked incapable of getting the ball under control. Every time he got it, he just launched it out of play. Gradually he settled down and became more confident and more commanding. He's such a force at the back and makes my job a lot easier.

February 22

We are always hot on morale and at training on Thursdays there is a ritual which keeps us all amused. We play a match among ourselves and it doesn't pay to be on the losing side. The losers have to do a forfeit, ten push-ups or sit-ups, whatever the winners decide. But then it gets personal. The winners get to choose a worst player from the losing side. For the unlucky man, it means handing over £20 to buy next week's papers plus three magazines of his choice. I have been voted for once or twice. 'Blakey' gets chosen for complaining all the time. Blakey and Hunt take it personally and seriously, so we wind them up as frequently as we can. Hunt once produced his £20 from his sock. Greg Halford was voted worst player on his first day, our view being that if he cost the club £2 million, he can afford it. Some people always seem to get away with it. Most of all we want to nail Kevin Dillon for his crap refereeing, but he slides out.

February 24

Paul Barron, the Middlesbrough goalkeeping coach, has known me for 20 years, ever since I was an eager teenager with a full head of hair. Paul has invited me, Amanda and my parents to dinner at his house after today's game at the Riverside. Before the game I knock on his dressing room door just to say 'hello'. Paul asks me if Amanda and my parents are driving up and if they are well. I tell him they are and then he says, "Right, now f*** off."

After the game, hostilities over, we go to his house to discover my college coach Cliff McCrath, who, of course, married

Amanda and I, and John Richardson, my goalkeeping coach at Seattle Pacific University, who are fellow guests. Who would have thought it? It's fantastic to see them again, but at 9.15pm we leave for home.

From left to right: Cliff McCrath, the coach of my SPU university side, Me, John Richardson, another coach at SPU, and Paul Barron at the Riverside.

Earlier...

Any team which has Mark Viduka and Yakubu as its front two ought to be challenging for everything. Viduka is a great player. He beats me with a back heel with his back to goal. It looks cheeky on television, but he actually got a bad touch and I tried to spread myself in case he turned. I guess I was four yards out and I should have dived at his feet. But it's easy to say that now. Viduka is so strong and he has this capacity to get into position early and it's hard to get the ball off him once he has possession. He reads the game so well and so quickly. I think sometimes it's best to let him have the ball and work at stopping players running off him. As for Yakubu, he has pace and power. He smashed a

A great view of the Viduka goal
- perhaps I should have dived at his feet.

shot past me with his left foot. When those two play like that, you wonder why Middlesbrough are below us. But they are. John Oster gets our goal, but we lose 2-1.

February 25

I find I watch football on television with a new interest this season. I really enjoy the televised games now that we are in the Premier League. In previous years I could take it or leave it. I didn't make a special effort to watch *Match of the Day*, for instance, but now I do. I find I'm looking at it from the coaching perspective, which is something I never expected to do. "Dad, you doing your homework?" one of the boys once said to me and I probably was.

I go with some friends today, mostly Chelsea fans and including Justin Chancellor of Tool, to Cardiff to see the Carling Cup final between Arsenal and their team. I find myself watching it from a coach's point of view, analysing and studying tactics. I guess in previous years I was not much interested in the Premier

League because I was so far removed from it. But now I'm living this dream and the season has so far been so exciting. It gets me thinking. I'm 35 in the summer and while that's not old for a goalkeeper, I have to look to the future. One day I'd like to coach. Where or when, I don't know, but for the first time I can see myself coaching, and that's not something I would have considered a year or two back.

At the Carling Cup final with (from the left)
Justin Chancellor, Craig Duffy and my Dad.

FEBRUARY 07

February 26

Other Sundays I devote to the family if I can. Sometimes there's a game of golf with Murts or Sal, but I like to clear the mind of football for a day. We go for bike rides as a family, but the boys are really into football now and like me to play along with them in the garden. I've always resisted the idea of forcing the game on them. I am happy for them to come to it naturally, but Amanda and I have always been prepared for the fact that they might find other things to do with their time. But they love it, play it at school and cheer their Dad from their seats on match days.

Even so, I was pleased when Austin, who's seven, asked me for goalkeeper training the other day. Hunter, who's just under a couple of years older, also plays in goal, but I think Austin is the keener to emulate his Dad at this stage. Hunter has this terrific left foot, which is not something he's inherited from me, in fact we have to work on his right. Austin dives around his goal crazily and makes some unbelievable saves at times. One time I'll always remember, Hunter let go a great left foot shot and goalkeeper Austin dived across to make an incredible block.

Amanda writes....

The boys have been going to matches since they were babies, so it's become a way of life. At their age they don't yet appreciate the quality of football they see. They play football in school, in the garden and on Saturday mornings and love it so much that going to watch their father in the afternoon is not quite as important to them as it used to be. As much as they love seeing Marcus in action, I think they would rather be playing in their own matches now.

February 27

Manchester United are back in town for the second time this season, to the surprise of everyone. After drawing at Old Trafford a week or two ago, there are no complaints now about Steve Coppell's team selection policy. I'm on the bench again and young Adam must play in front of a live television audience in only his fourth match. It's odd being a substitute, you get the chance to look at the crowd and take it all in. If you play, you only see what's in front. What I see now is three United goals in just about the first ten minutes. I remember thinking, "Here we go, this could get ugly." On the bench we were all looking at each other and saying, "What the hell's happening?" If you go three goals down to a team with United's strengths you're looking at a big, big defeat. But it never happens. The famous Reading team spirit kicks in and in the end the width of a crossbar prevents the match going into extra-time. From 3-0 we get it back to 3-2 and at least we go out of the FA Cup with our heads held high.

Mentor and pupil - with Adam Federici.

February 28

The problem is Federici gets hammered on television and in the Press today for letting in what looked like soft goals and I feel bad about it for him. The first looked the worst because a low shot beat him after Shorey had taken a swing at it to try and clear. If you don't see the ball until it's too late because some other player is in your way, as Shorey was, there is nothing any keeper in the world can do about it. Without the player in front of him, Federici would have saved it 100 times out of 100.

FEBRUARY 07

The second goal from Louis Saha was an unbelievable effort across the keeper's body. Once the ball hits the ground just in front of you, it's a nightmare for keepers. That also shows the level we are at now. Those sort of guys can shoot like that all day. The third goal was just a great finish, but Federici recovered his poise later and makes a decent save or two. I went up to him at the final whistle. "Stuff happens," I say. He's just disappointed, his Dad was in the crowd again, and later we talk through the goals, but no-one is critical of him; except those in the media.

Enjoying being in the Actim Team of the Week once again.
The Premiership has proved to be a real dreamland so far.

MARCH

07

The boys at the Emirates Stadium.

March 3

Ever since Arsenal moved into the Emirates Stadium I've been looking forward to playing there. I get tickets for some neighbours and for Andy, the golf pro at Sandford Springs Golf Club, and his son. I would like to think Andy will be supporting us, but that's the trouble with a place like Reading, where there's no tradition of big-time football, a lot of people back Manchester United, Arsenal and top teams like that and it's easy to get to London. The stadium is every bit as fantastic as I hoped it would be. There's a lull in the game and it gives me the chance to look around and take it in. The big screens suddenly list the teams and there's my name. I find the whole experience unbelievable. I shake my head and take a swig of Red Bull. Never in my widest dreams did I ever think I would end up somewhere like this, but you never know where life's going to take you. It's a sweet moment. Not so sweet is the result, we lose 2-1. Arsenal get a penalty, the ref reckons Andre Bikey has fouled one of their players, but I'm not so sure. Forwards are taught to get themselves fouled in tight situations, so now it's me versus Gilberto from the spot. I always fancy my chances with penalties and I should have got this one. I get a finger tip to it but in fairness Gilberto takes it well, all along the ground, and had it been a few inches higher I'm sure I would have reached it. For a fraction of a second I think I'm going to succeed. But once again we've gained a ton of respect from the opposition including, I find out later, from Arsène Wenger. We also pick up some sympathy, which I reckon is because we are so obviously the underdogs and everyone roots for the underdog. Last year the nation was saying, "Come on Wigan", but they are old Premier League hands compared to us now. Next year we might have the same kind of problem.

Saving from Theo Walcott at the Emirates.

March 4

I met Jens Lehmann after the game yesterday. I find him an intriguing guy. In fact, it's the third time I've met him and we get on well. The first was when the United States played Germany and we've built up a relationship. "Reading. Your guys are doing well," he said to me. The purpose was to get his shirt for my collection, but I have to be wary because Amanda is looking for items for a race night and auction tomorrow night and I wouldn't want that to get in there.

March 5

The shirt's gone missing. Yes, it's an auction item and, yes, I have to buy it back. Don't ask me how much I pay.

Amanda writes......

Race nights are great fun and you don't have to be an expert to be a winner. Sue Roberts sets it up at the Madejski Stadium and there are 400 or more people and there's a pleasant, casual atmosphere. A lot of players are into racing, Glen Little for one, and Kevin Doyle's family have ponies and know a bit about horses. Not that any knowledge of horses is required. The races are pre-recorded so anyone can win. You can bet on horses, sponsor horses, races and jockeys. It all adds up. We have a great evening, lots of shouting, and the final count is another £17,000. There's an auction, of course, and Marcus gets his shirt back plus one or two other items which caught his eye. We've actually exceeded the figure we set ourselves, but the Royals Families decide not to nominate any new charities at the moment or to distribute any money just yet.

The Royals Families girls at the Race Night. From left to right, back row: Hrefna (Ivar Ingimarsson's wife), Karen Murty, Sasha (Shane Long's girlfriend), Jenny Harney (Kevin Doyle's girlfriend), Amanda, Olga (Bryn Gunnarsson's wife), Claire Hollowell (Dave Kitson's girlfriend). Front row: Krystell Sidwell, Emily Shorey, Sarah Little.

March 7

Some newspaper guy called Oliver Holt had a go at us a while back, criticising the club and the chairman in a column he writes. He accused John Madejski of having a giant ego, naming the stadium after himself, and saying Reading were a nice little middle class club not to be taken seriously. I think he believed Stephen Hunt had deliberately kicked Petr Cech. Sure, we saw what he'd written and wondered what the chairman had done to upset him. Holt seems to be courting controversy and we laugh at his outburst, a little surprised he's bothered himself with us. Something had got under his skin. None of the players care, but I know a few fans respond angrily when Holt came on a local radio phone-in. The chairman didn't deserve the criticism, but if you're in the public eye you have to be prepared for the occasional attack. I find him to be a pleasant guy and what many people don't realise is that the football team means a lot to him. He's at most away games and the club is part of him. I see him match days and he's always friendly and approachable. I can't think why anyone would want to attack him. As for the name of our stadium, it's worth millions these days to any company to have theirs associated with a Premier League club, but it was not worth anything when it was built.

John Madejski, the Chairman, was the subject of an undeserved vitriolic attack in a national newspapaper.

March 8

Andre Bikey has done great lately. I've never come across a guy on the phone as much as he is, and always speaking Spanish. I guess it shows how cosmopolitan we are as a club. He's a big guy and it's not been easy for him to adapt after his time in Russia, but he's learning all the time too. We saw evidence of his potential on the pre-season tour of Sweden, but he almost cost himself a move when he got himself sent off in one of the friendlies. He's comfortable on the ball, sometimes just a little too comfortable for my liking, but he'll get over that.

March 9

We get to play only two Premier League matches in 28 days this month just when the season should be reaching some sort of climax. I don't know how this has developed but there's a bunch of internationals going on and we lose players to them as other clubs are doing. Training's a bit quiet, but I'm wondering again about my own international career. I have to say that playing internationals is now a nice bonus for me, nothing more. I'm playing every week at Reading in the Premier League and while I like the idea of playing for my country, having had such a super time at the World Cup, my body might not be up to it in the long term. The hip hurts and in dark moments I figure I may not be able to play much longer if it's not sorted out, so I have to look after myself. I'm used to international rejection. I played in three games for the USA when I was at Seattle and then nothing for those eight years, five months and 28 days until 2003. Then suddenly, after all those years of being forgotten when I thought my chances had gone, I was chosen to face New Zealand in Richmond and we won 2-1. Why they called me up after all that time, I'm still not sure. Then I had to wait another two years, until July 2005, before, best of all, I got to play in the 2005 Gold Cup win against Cuba in front of my home crowd in Seattle. My (so far) last international was against Guatemala in a World Cup qualifier in September 2005. I hope I don't have to wait another eight years, but Bob Bradley will notice what I do for Reading, so nothing is ruled out. Anyway, I have a simple philosophy. If I never play another day at any level, I would have been a success. I feel I have cheated life so far. I'm playing in the best league in the world and if anything else happens, it happens. I have a laid back attitude and I love it.

March 10

David Beckham looks like he's heading for America and one or two media outlets have been on to me to get my opinion. At this stage I have sort of mixed feelings. LA Galaxy will sign him when his Real Madrid contract ends in the summer unless there's a last minute change of mind. For a start he's going to raise the profile of soccer, as it's known there, in the United States. Asian countries are buying the TV rights in anticipation, so Galaxy and the MLS will get their money back, but the standard is going to be well below what he's been used to in England and Spain. I had a feeling he would go to America, partly because I couldn't imagine him coming back to England. The States was definitely his best option. What he has to remember is that some of his teammates and opponents are on about 30,000 dollars a year and might not take kindly to a superstar like him, on massive wages, coming in on their territory. I have no fears he will be well protected. He's strong and he's smart and he'll look after himself. It helps also that in the MLS, referees quickly give fouls for what would just be heavy tackles over here. One thing I should warn him about, though, is when he gets to play in places like Dallas it can reach 115 degrees in the height of the summer.

The flow of talent is still most likely to be the other way. Goochie Onyewu has recently signed for Newcastle after doing well in the World Cup. Good guy, Goochie. He's super strong and I think he will make the grade over here once he's settled. I thought we might have shown some interest in him. As for Beckham, he will sell shirts and get more people in the stadiums.

He is one of the biggest names in world football and it's a great boost for the American game in prospect.

March 16

Tomorrow our long run without a competitive game is interrupted when we play at home to Portsmouth. I always look forward to seeing friends again among the goalkeeping fraternity. First choice at Portsmouth is David James, whom I came across briefly when I was on a sort of trial at Aston Villa, coming over from America. He's having a great season, save after save, match after match. I'm not surprised. He's had a great career because one of his main qualities is that he's super quick. But he has everything else. Some say he should have played more often for England in his prime, but David Seaman kept him out for so long. It was hard for him to get games and I know the feeling. Friedel, Keller and Tony Meola were always in front of me, and you can't ask for a transfer. The other guy I shall be pleased to see is Jamie Ashdown, who was my number two at Reading before he left for Portsmouth. Jamie's from the Reading area and played ten games in a row when I was injured, but realised he had to take his chance and get away. It was a gamble. Sure, the money was better, but I know he wanted to show what he could do. He got in the team down there and was close to becoming first choice, but then hurt his back and now he's stuck behind James. I liked Jamie Ashdown, we worked together and I watched him develop. In football things can change quickly.

March 17

When we last played Portsmouth in October they were on fire and they deserved to beat us. It was one of the few games where we have been beaten by more than one goal and it was not one of our best matches. I remember thinking what a great player Kanu still is and Portsmouth seem to specialise in getting the last drop out of guys who other clubs thought were finished. Sol Campbell and David James are typical and Linvoy Primus is a hard man to get past. They're super solid, James makes tons of saves and there is a self-belief about them in the same way there is a self-belief about us. I know his critics keep on about James's occasional blunders but Harry Redknapp has got him playing. Today we are still not at our best and a goalless draw is about right. They hit a post, but then James shows why he's the only keeper in front of me in the Actim Index. Perhaps with us two playing it's no surprise there are no goals. I'm happy with the clean sheet, but collectively we are not as fluent as we are normally.

March 18

I was in Starbucks in Reading one time and recognised an American accent. "You American?" I said to this guy. He was, and so began a family friendship with Scott Allison, at the time coach of the Bracknell Bees ice hockey team. Scott and his wife had kids the same age as ours, so we saw quite a bit of each other until they went back to America. Scott was a monster, he was always showing off new cuts and bruises, but through him I went to watch the Bees when I could. I can ice skate and of course hockey's a big sport in the States. I was watching them practice one day when the goalie had to go off for treatment and Scott told me to put the pads on. I was just a little worried about this. If I too got injured, how would I explain that away to Steve Coppell? It's a dangerous sport and goalies are not protected by referees. But at least the padding they wear is effective and I thought I'd give it a go. I had blockers on one hand and a glove on the other and suddenly shots were raining in on me from all angles. It was as much as I could do just to stand up but in a funny kind of way I enjoyed the experience. If you're a keeper in one sport, it's natural to think you might be able to play in that position in another. So Scott was my connection to the Bracknell Bees and even when he went home to the States, I continued to follow their fortunes. Today they have asked me to make a presentation and I'm only too happy to do it. The Bees have had a fantastic

At the Bracknell Bees' stadium presenting
the English Premier Hockey League trophy.

season and are national champions. I put on a Bees shirt and I'm pleased to hand over the English Premier Ice Hockey League trophy to the squad. They deserved their success.

March 19

Football is being seen as a means of connecting with kids who are either not reading at school or not reading enough. If they can be induced to read about football it might lead to them reading about other subjects. Each Premier League club is invited to supply an ambassador for the league's Reading Stars campaign to encourage reading. Sara, who does community work at Reading Football Club, asks me if I would become our ambassador and I'm happy to do it. Each ambassador had to choose a couple of books, one for adults and one for kids. I have always read for fun when the opportunity is there. It's hard to get stuck into a thriller on the team bus but sometimes in hotels it's possible to get a book out in quiet moments. The books I have chosen reflect my own interests. My top book is Tom Clancy's *Without Remorse*. I first read it for fun and there's a lot of technical stuff and information in it which I kind of enjoy. For children, my pick was *The Gruffalo*, which I loved as a kid and which I have read to mine. They love it too. If any of this helps, then great.

March 20

On match days I shave my head as part of the ritual I employ. It's something I've been doing ever since about 1996 and I can't see that changing. It started at Denver when I was playing for Colorado Rapids when one of the guys said I would look even meaner if I shaved my head. I thought about it, but did nothing until one day we had our pictures taken for a newspaper. The story was that seven wives of the Rapids' players were pregnant at the same time. Each player stood behind their seated wife. To my horror, when the picture appeared, it made me look bald.

From that day I decided to shave my head. But I have to say that even if I allowed it to grow, there would not be much left.

March 23

Amanda writes.....

Today I'm one of many people taking part in the Green Park Challenge, a little three-mile run which ends at the Madejski Stadium. The big event of the day is the Reading Half-Marathon and the stadium is filled with friends and relatives, all cheering and shouting their favourite among the thousands of participants over the finishing line and it's quite a scene. This was how I first came to see Reading. The Reading Half-Marathon is a few weeks before the London Marathon and some athletes use it as it as a warm-up. That's what I did in 2002. I entered and took part in both. At the time we were well settled in Wimbledon, as opposed to many Americans, who headed home after 9/11, their departure making those of us who remained a little uneasy.

I remember 9/11 vividly. We were used to planes coming in low over London bound for Heathrow, but that day the skies were eerily quiet. I know there is the stigma of the ugly American abroad, but I think that overall there is a great sense of goodwill towards the USA and those Americans who, like us, live in their midst. Marcus's transfer to Reading from Fulham went through in August 2002 and we had to move out of London and find somewhere near Reading to live. Marcus scoured the internet for houses and drove past those he liked the look of, but it was not going to be an easy task because neither of us had any local knowledge. We found Starbucks and Costco very reassuring, and then one day Marcus told me to get down to a village called Pangbourne, near the River Thames, because he had spotted somewhere I might like. I did. It was in a quiet area and what did it for us was spotting from outside in a window of the house we wanted to buy a Seattle Mariners baseball pennant. We were sure it was an omen. The selling family had been out there. But what

Above and below: We have taken part in the Green Park
Challenge as a family on several occasions.

MARCH 07

really clinched it for us was that neither of us could get a mobile reception. The same thing had happened in our previous two homes, so we figured we had to buy. A few years down the line, this is the most settled I have ever been. Maybe the age of our kids helps because the parents of their friends have become our friends, but the whole area is just great for us. We have street parties in the summer with bunting across the road and some of the older people act as pseudo grandparents to Hunter and Austin. There's a big mix of ages, the kids love their school and Marcus and I feel part of the community. When you move you want to experience the place and the people and at the moment I feel like we live in England. We have plenty of friends and family come over to see us. I point them to our rail station and I tell them Oxford is half an hour north and London half an hour east. But I suppose Seattle is fundamentally home for us. The kids have cousins over there, our parents are there and our school friends will be friends for life. Hunter and Austin associate Seattle with summer and fun, as I have said, so we wonder what might happen in a few years. When Marcus and I go back we both notice how commercially over the top the United States has become. I think we might even struggle to re-settle if we decide to go back permanently. As for the Green Park Challenge, I do that in about 20 or so minutes, nothing special.

March 24

My mother-in-law is in touch again. She's spotted my name as best Premiership goalkeeper of the week and wastes no time in telling me. There are lots of different parameters but it shows I'm doing my job in a good team. The whole team is doing well and it's incredible how many qualities there are about every one of us. I'm pleased, of course, for the individual recognition, but there are many deserving cases in the Reading team.

March 27

I'm off to Buckingham Palace today to meet the Queen. I can hardly believe I've just said that, but it's true. Out of nowhere an invitation arrives in the post to attend a reception at the Palace. At first I thought it was some kind of joke, but I later discover I'm one of 300 to 400 prominent Americans living in Britain who get the same invitation. There are military people, businessmen, actors and a sprinkling of footballers. Eddie Lewis is there, as are both Brian McBride and Carlos Bocagnegra, representatives of the growing number now living and working in the United Kingdom. The Queen is due to make a short visit to the United States shortly and this is some sort of run up to it. I have to wear a suit over my cowboy boots and get checked to see if I'm carrying a bomb. There's champagne and good wine and it's a wonderful occasion. Prince Philip, smaller than I imagined, but now well into his 80s, remarks that he is surprised how many Americans are playing soccer in England and asks about the standard of the game in the USA. I also speak briefly to the Queen, who is charming and pleasant. But she doesn't mention my royals and I don't ask about hers.

March 28

In the absence of any fixtures I have to work at my game as if there's a match on Saturday. You have to be able to use both feet these days and while I can get big distances with my right, my left needs constant work. Sal does his best, but we both know I'm good for a 'shank' at some time or other. My guys are on the touchlines waiting for me to find them, but it could go anywhere. I always try to hit the ball to perfection, but then it goes out of play. Sometimes my worst kicks are the best because they deceive everyone, me included. Punching is something I practice because it's vital and a goalkeeper's big weapon against the balls they use these days, which I'm always complaining about. Technique and timing are all-important with the emphasis on a short, sharp jab since the balls whipped into the danger area often have so much pace on them.

One of the key jobs for any goalkeeper now is to organise the players in front of him and I'm no different. Communication is absolutely vital, telling guys where they should be standing, making them aware if an opponent is moving into their zone. It keeps you on your game, but the problem in the Premier League is that the crowds are so loud, so you might as well be speaking to yourself at times. I keep the orders to a minimum when it gets too loud. "Step up" is an important command, "Keepers" tells defenders it's my ball and "Head it to me" is pretty crucial too.

As for goal celebrations, it's become a ritual among our players to race to the touchline and crash into Kingsley, the Reading lovable lion mascot. Murty made a spectacle of himself hugging the mascot after his penalty against Queen's Park Rangers, but it's all too far away for me. By the time I get up there, everyone else is running around, the celebrations nearly over. I content myself with a couple of clenched fist salutes and some caffeine from a can of Red Bull. It energises me and helps me stay focused and concentrated. As for the mascot, he must go home bruised some days.

One of the rare occasions when I managed to reach
Kingsley Royal before the rest of the team.

Modelling my new kit. It was the boots that worried me though!

APRIL

07

All for one and one for all.

April 1

This is going to sound like an April Fool's joke, but I've run into trouble for drinking Red Bull. Just as I'm preparing for the game at Tottenham, I'm told that Lucozade, the Premier League's official sports drink partner, have spotted me swigging Red Bull, one of their rivals, I guess, in my goal during games and they're not happy. Red Bull is part of my pre-match ritual, which I have explained is so important to me, and I have been drinking the sugar-free variety for three years. It's important to me and I'm baffled as to what to do. I want to carry on drinking Red Bull, but I don't want to upset Lucozade, who put big money into our game. For the Spurs game I pour Red Bull into a Lucozade bottle and put that into the back of my net, but it tastes vile from the plastic bottle. I won't do that again. For the rest of the season my plan is to put white tape around the Red Bull logo. We'll see if it works.

Earlier...

Paul Robinson, the Tottenham goalkeeper, scored a freak goal against Watford a couple of weeks ago. His big kick bounced over

Ben Foster and into the net and Foster was made to look a little foolish. I've never been caught out like that, but, as you'll know from reading this book, I'm wary of the faster balls they use these days. Nike balls are the best in my opinion. But it gets me thinking, I can kick big distances with my right foot and wouldn't it be great to get a Premiership goal?!

Despite my injury I make a couple of good saves, including this one from Rocha.

Later...

My ambition to play every minute of every Premiership game comes to an end today. In training the day before, I landed awkwardly on my right foot pushing off and the muscles around my hip hurt. I iced the injury, it improved and there was no question of me missing the match. But a few minutes into the game at White Hart Lane, I felt it again and it got worse and worse. In fact I made a couple of good saves, so it wasn't obvious I was struggling, but when we got back to the dressing room at half-time I knew I wouldn't be going back out for the second half.

I hoped it might loosen up over 15 or 20 minutes of the break, but there was nothing the physio could do. The gaffer said: "Don't risk it" and I know he was right. It's a shame because I wanted to play the whole league season, in itself an achievement, so I guess I'll have to start again next year.

Robbie Keane beats me from the penalty spot for the only goal of the game at White Hart Lane.

April 2

As members of the Professional Footballers' Association, and I'm an active member, we get to vote for Player of the Year and Young Player of the Year. I have no doubts about where my votes are going. Ronaldo is head and shoulders above everyone else, apart maybe from Drogba, so he's my Player of the Year. My Young Player of the Year is Cesc Fabregas of Arsenal. I love watching Fabregas and in a year or two he'll be challenging for the top prize. Later this month there's a dinner and presentations in London, one of the social highlights of the season. I'll be there.

April 4

Amanda writes.......

We have a fashion show today and there's plenty of enthusiasm from the players, the Royal Families and the stores and shops of Reading, mainly those in the Oracle Centre, who have contributed so readily in terms of clothes and outfits. Jenny Harney and Olga, Bryn Gunnarsson's wife, are the main organisers with help from Jo Doyle. Marcus is not a model today, but Ronnie Grant, the kitman, is and gets some abuse from Marcus and Karen Murty, who are sitting near the catwalk. There's hair and make-up to be done and a lot of time and effort goes into it all. The men show off some casual wear including Diesel leisure clothing and it all goes well. Among the players and staff there are some natural models. Sonko takes off his shirt, Wally Downes rips the back of his trousers to great laughter and our kitman looks good in a classic button-down shirt. The whole evening raises another £12,000.

We've decided to support two extra charities because of the success in our previous fund-raising activities. Tonight was for Daisy's Dream, for bereaved children, and the Thames Valley and Chiltern Air Ambulance Trust, a charity also supported by the Oracle Shopping Centre. Our total sum of money brought in by the Royals Families now tops £100,000.

Marcus writes...

I sold some raffle tickets and recorded the whole event with the club video camera. It's a bit different, a great laugh and the money's rolling in. Fantastic!

April 7

I didn't train until Thursday and didn't start kicking until Friday. The hip hurts, but I'm taking a chance. Liverpool at home is one of the biggest matches of the season and I want to play in it. Even warming up at the end where there's little or no grass in the goalmouth, I'm wary about making a false move. Liverpool win 2-1 and I get my only booking of the season for handling outside the area. Some papers say I should have got a red. It's late in the game and Dirk Kuyt chased down a long ball. I ran to the edge of my area and sort of clawed the ball down. I didn't know at the time if I was in or outside the area. The ref decided I'm out and Liverpool were screaming for me to be sent off, so I was pretty relieved when I got only a yellow. The ref put the ball down for a free-kick on the edge of the area, Gerrard took it and Hunty headed the ball off the goal line. So I've got away with it.

Kuyt scores the winner for Liverpool at the Madejski.

In retrospect I should have headed the ball as I ran out, but there's only ever a split second to make a decision like that and it's easy to say that now.

April 9

It's Easter and the matches are coming thick and fast. We're at Charlton today, not having won for five league matches and seven in all. Once again some of our fans are concerned about our results. "Are you struggling?" I was asked by one. "No, we are not," is the answer. None of us feel any different and there's no sense of panic or despondency. It's not as easy as people think. We have to be at 100 per cent all the time, individually and as a unit, and sometimes it's just not your day, no matter how well you play.

Reading fans at Charlton.
Despite our indifferent form of late they have turned out
in their numbers and voiced great support.

Later...

Charlton are in trouble, fighting for their lives. Alan Pardew is manager there now and he's finding it hard. Pards is a character, we know him well having been a former manager at Reading and he was trying to put off some of our players with his comments from the touchline, but that was never going to work. I had a great game, not that you would know from the average marks I get next morning in the papers. There was a whole bunch of crosses to deal with and I made a couple of good saves, if I say so myself. I came off feeling really good about my game and I was pumped up for some time afterwards.

Sal and I analysed all the moves and when I see it again on television later, I can't help but I feel I've done well. But the next day in the papers, and on that night's *Match of the Day*, it's all about Charlton. The saves I make are blamed on poor finishing and I'm annoyed that my efforts are not properly recognised. But that's life. The talk is about the top two and the bottom six and the rest of us are just making up the numbers, it seems.

April 10

For some reason we at Reading have been drug-tested a lot. I don't know why. Do they think Steve Coppell is dishing out some magic potion? It's supposed to be random, but it doesn't seem like that. We always get to be chosen for the televised games. Names are drawn out of a hat and the 'lucky' player has to give a urine sample after the game. Sounds simple, but it's not so straightforward as Andre Bikey discovered after the Charlton game. I've had to take my turn in the past and let's just say it's easier for a goalkeeper to perform than an outfield player. We run around less and don't dehydrate as quickly. Anyway, poor Andre could not provide his sample as the rest of us got dressed and prepared to board the coach home. For an hour we sat on that bus, the engine running, waiting for Andre to do his stuff, but it just wouldn't happen. In the end the decision was made to go home. Andre's wife was summoned to keep him company as the rest of us left the stadium. I'm told it was another hour before he was able to provide his sample.

April 11

Leroy Lita's been banned for three matches on the basis of television evidence. The FA have decided he head-butted El Karkouri at Charlton and pronounce the suspension. The ref saw nothing at the time and even television is not conclusive. Lits is very upset. He plays with super intensity, as Roy Keane did for all those years. I don't play that way. I play better when relaxed. If I'm in a collision, I usually help the other guy to his feet, but that's me. Lits is better when he's fired up and I know how frustrated and disappointed he is. He's missed a big portion of the season already for one reason or another and is just coming into form. He just wants to play and this has set him back. I think he's been unlucky. It wasn't much of a clash and his opponent made the most of it.

Giving a shirt to a fan after the game at the Valley.

April 12

Sidwell is getting linked with everybody now and the club are letting all the speculation run. You can't blame him for seeing what options there are out there. He's a commodity. He's giving everything and has more reasons to keep doing the right things than most of us because people are watching him and wondering. I want him to stay, we all do. Would I do the same as him if I was in his position? Probably. Basically, if your club doesn't give you the money you want, you leave if you can get a better deal elsewhere. That's a fact of life in any profession. Why should football be any different?

April 13

We play at home to Fulham tomorrow and they're another club in trouble. I don't like to see them struggling, but my only concern is to beat them. It didn't happen for me at Fulham. I couldn't get into the team because Maik Taylor was playing so well and then along came Edwin van der Sar. In my first year there I was going to play in the last couple of games, but I gashed a knee and in my second year I was again on the bench for much of the time, though I did play against Northampton twice in the cup and Sheffield Wednesday and Grimsby in the league. We were promoted that year and they got me a championship medal and, in fairness, Jean Tigana looked after me well. There were some great players at Craven Cottage at the time, Saha, Malbranque, Clark, Coleman, Boa Morte, Hayles, Horsfield, Sean Davis, Goldbaek, Reidle, Collins and Finnan.

My contract ran out after van der Sar joined, but Tigana was good enough to give me week-to-week contracts to help me look around. I tried out at Coventry, Walsall and Middlesbrough, but then Reading came in for me and I leapt at the chance. I had spent a few games on loan at Reading, which I'd really enjoyed, but feared the collapse of ITV Digital might mean they couldn't afford to sign me permanently. But two games into the season,

Pards called me up and I couldn't sign fast enough. The stadium was great, it was not far from London and within another game or two I had displaced Phil Whitehead as number one goalkeeper.

It was the best and luckiest decision of my footballing life. But then the way they scouted me was pretty weird too. One night I found myself on the bench for a reserve team match in the days when Fulham played at Wimbledon. I didn't mind since I would rather be on the bench for the reserves than at home watching TV. Maik Taylor, who had been devastated by van der Sar's arrival, was playing and he asked me to help warm him up. I was happy to do that and, luckily, Kevin Dillon and Brian McDermott, Reading's backroom staff, watched me kicking the ball and preparing generally and went back to Pards and said, in effect, "Sign this man". I think my kicking was a key factor in the decision.

April 14

I'm sorry to see Chris Coleman has paid the penalty for Fulham's recent failures. I really warmed to Chris as a player and as a person. He could be super funny, but he was also a great captain and it was no surprise to me when he later became manager. We were friends and I used to meet him for a coffee or two at Starbucks in Wimbledon. I was actually with him earlier on the day of his very bad accident which ended his career and almost killed him. It was a huge shock to hear of his injuries and he did well to come back from them to lead a normal life.

Later...

We win 1-0 at home to Fulham and I make a couple of good saves, one of them, pleasingly, from Brian McBride. It's my second successive shut-out and we're looking like our old selves again. I can admit it now, but I really wanted to impress against my old club and I hadn't realised just how much until after the match when I was super pumped up. A win would have lifted Fulham nearer safety, but it never happened for them and I can see how dejected they are. I have some American buddies on the other side - Clint Dempsey, McBride, Carlos Bocanegra - and I don't want friends to be relegated.

April 18/19

Amanda writes...

The Royals Families work goes on. Everyone who reads about our activities and the way we are raising funds wants to join in or help in some way. On the 18th, for instance, the Star Supporters' Trust organised for us a quiz night at the Crowne Plaza in Reading and that nets another £2,000, for which we are grateful. The following night Karen Murty and I speak at a Rotary Club dinner, telling local businessmen of our aims and ambitions and how we came into being. I was a little nervous, but I got through it without too many mistakes, I hope, and again we were received with great enthusiasm.

April 21

A goalkeeper always knows his angles. To not signals a lack of control. I mention this only because at Bolton today we concede a super soft own goal. I can't ever bring myself to criticise Nick Shorey, who must have run 70 yards to get back when Bolton broke away from the halfway line. The Bolton player shot across me, I could see the ball was going wide, but then Nick slides in behind me and puts it in our net. Shorey's been just fantastic all season, but the weird part of all this is that in my opinion if he had not scored for them to make it 1-0 we would not have gone on and won 3-1.

Steve Coppell changed our formation to 4-3-3 when we were up against it. Until that goal I was having a good day, catching some difficult crosses and making a save or two, but I was truly gutted when they went ahead like that. But the manager always knows when to change things and when Shane Long came on as a substitute, the game swung our way. I guess Bolton were surprised when we equalised, but they could never have expected us to come back the way we did.

I'm claiming assists for our second and third goals, but I must be honest about our last. We were 2-1 up and time was running out. I was debating whether to hump the ball down the pitch to waste time or throw it to Shorey on the left to waste time. I decided on the latter. Shorey made his way down the pitch deep into their territory and I was shouting: "Do not cross the ball, do not cross that ball!" at him. I feared their keeper would collect it and kick it back down into our danger area.

But Shorey did cross it…I was just about to swear at him and what happens? Hunty emerges from nowhere to score. As I say, what do I know?

Later…

I ring my buddy Ray Northway. He's been at a wedding where he was told we're losing 1-0. The line's not too good. I tell him we've won 3-1 and he doesn't hear it properly. He goes back to the wedding thinking we've lost 3-1.

April 22

It's the night of the PFA dinner and presentation at the Grosvenor House Hotel in central London. For me, it's black tie and cowboy boots. My choice Ronaldo is named Player of the Year and he is also voted Young Player of the Year. Ronaldo's a great player. Manchester United have eight players in the PFA team of the year, including the whole back five, Chelsea have only one. I voted for van der Sar in the team category, but the voting was done in March when United were walking away with the title. Later it got closer. I know what it feels like to be named in a representative team. Last year I was in the PFA Championship Team of the Year and people don't realise how big

At the PFA Awards night - it's a suit and dicky bow this time!!

a deal that is. To be recognised by your fellow professionals as the best is an incredible honour and it really is as good as it gets. Your opponents only see you twice a year to judge you and the award is something to show for the pride I place in being super consistent.

What pleases me most about tonight is seeing Kevin Doyle among the nominations for Young Player of the Year. I'm incredibly proud of him because the competition is intense. There's a lot of good young players out there - Ronaldo, Rooney, Fabregas, Wright-Phillips - but there he is, up among them. Two seasons ago he was coming over from Ireland unheard of and, while I think he's deserved his honour, it's still a bit surprising. I didn't get over here until I was 28 or 29, so I'm a latecomer to all this, but Kevin has come on a bundle and will get even better.

It's hard to recognise some of these household names in dinner suits and a lot of time is spent trying to work out who they are without their team shirts on and names on their back. But it's a great night.

April 23

Steve Coppell is saying we don't want to be in Europe and I'm surprised it's caused such a stir. Why would we not want to be in Europe? Of course we want to play in the UEFA Cup next season. It would be the next step up for those many of us who have never played in international club competition. All Steve has ever said so far is that we couldn't consider Europe all the while we were making absolutely certain of not being relegated. He never said we were not interested in it. Sure, we never talked of Europe, but only because we had other priorities. The manager has always emphasised the next match, nothing further. I know all footballers say this, but we really do concentrate on each match as it comes along. This way there's no extra pressure. Only now, as the season nears its end, is Steve able to say, "Yes, we would like to play in Europe if we are good enough to qualify."

April 25

Amanda writes...

I love golf, so helping to run a golf day as our next major Royals Families event was something I enjoyed. We chose Sandford Springs Golf Club and it all went smoothly again. Many of the Reading footballers took part and we teamed them with those people who had bought sponsorship. Steve Coppell really enjoys his golf and he played his 18 holes with great enthusiasm. The day began with bacon rolls and, after the rounds had been completed, there was a sit-down meal, auction and raffle. At the end of it all our charities were £11,000 better off.

Since this was our last big fund-raiser of the season, we found that at the end of it all we had got together over £100,000 for dispersal, way more than I ever expected at the outset. We've decided that our two nominated charities would get £30,000 each, as we had promised, but the destination of the rest will be decided at the start of next season. It's been a fantastic effort and every member of the Royals Families has played a full part in what we have managed to achieve so far. While I was not surprised at the work put in by so many of the girls, who have been magnificent, I don't think I realised how supportive everyone would be.

April 30

We play Newcastle tonight and I have some new boots to wear courtesy of Nike. Brad Self, Nike's man in the United States, asks me to wear some new boots for the last two or three matches without telling me what colour they were. When I ask him about the colour, he gets a bit evasive. "I'll send a picture of them," he says, before making his excuses and ringing off. Black is my preferred choice, so when yellow ones arrive I'm a little taken aback. The match is being televised and I wonder what reaction it might provoke, but they're nice to wear and there are no blisters. I will be wearing black ones next season, but the yellow boots will be a reserve.

Later...

This morning all the papers were full of Michael Owen making his comeback after being out with that horrendous injury he picked up at the World Cup last summer for so long. But it overshadows everything. It's like Reading are just there to make up the numbers, but we've already got many more points than Newcastle. There's a lot of hype and I can't stop thinking about it, or Owen. The runs he makes are so good, he's always in the right spot, and that's what marks him out from lesser strikers. Inexperienced forwards are always getting offside and I don't think some of them realise how damaging that can be to their team. From the free kick, the opposition can be attacking in no time. Cunning guys like Owen test the linesmen by getting offside once or twice, but when he goes on a run he usually knows exactly what he's doing.

Later...

We win 1-0 and Dave Kitson gets our winner. He's had a miserable year because of injuries and this is a nice break for him. We've been lucky with our injuries so far in terms of forwards. Lits, Kitson and Doyle have all missed substantial parts of the season, but never together. When one of them was out, another came back, so it's worked out nicely. Kits is a good target man for my big kicks out of defence, excellent in the air, as Lits and Doyle are, and capable on the ground too. Kitson and I have played together a long time now, so we know each other's game well. He's a classic centre-forward, bigger than our other forwards, and a good finisher. We're pleased for him. What gives him an edge is the fact that, unlike so many footballers, he's had a job outside the game, in his case stacking shelves, I believe. Doing something like that gives him a perspective. As for Owen, I make an early save from him, but it's obvious he's still feeling his way.

A minute's silence - immaculately observed -
for Alan Ball before the Newcastle game.

APRIL 07

Dave Kitson celebrates his winner against Newcastle
- after all his injury problems it was great to see.

Facing up to an aerial challenge against Watford.
I was not happy we lost our last home game of the campaign.

"No slacking at the end of the season, boys!"

May 1

We have to vote for our Reading Player of the Year: the whole squad voting for a player we feel has stood out. It is not easy. It's a secret ballot, so I will never know if I'm alone in deciding on Brynjar Gunnarsson. Brynjar played centre-back, right-back and midfield at some point during the season and was super solid wherever Steve Coppell needed him. So many players were outstanding, but I just felt Brynjar's versatility somehow typified the whole team. Even if he came off the bench, he did us proud. He's one of those players who does not get the recognition they deserve because they are so unobtrusive, but the rest of the team notice, believe me.

The vote goes to Ivar Ingimarsson in the end and I'm happy with that. Ivar's had a great season and proved a few people wrong along the way. When Sonks was injured, they said Ivar would be exposed, but he never was. I think we actually had a better defensive record after Sonks than before. The point about the performance of the whole squad is that if just two or three of our players had done well over the whole year, we would have gone straight back down. But the spirit being what it was, all of us played to our maximum ability pretty much all of the time. That's the secret.

May 5

We are at home to Watford, who are already relegated, for our last game at the Madejski Stadium and I have a bad feeling about it. I can't decide if it's going to be a walk in the park or like facing Manchester United. It's a derby match of sorts and I'm sure they would like to beat us as a way of saying goodbye to the Premier League. We've always had close games with Watford, not necessarily exciting ones, but there has never been much in it. It's been a long season and getting up for another game, mentally, is strangely hard.

I complain to the referee about one of Watford's goals.

…Sure enough we pay for just a hint of complacency, Watford beat us 2-0 after we concede a soft goal and never recover. It was just not meant to be.

Later…

Okay, I admit it: I screwed up for one of the goals. An awkward cross comes in and I should have tipped it over and worried about the corner after that. But it's late in the match and I spot John Oster out of the corner of my eye, free on a wing. I want to counter attack, but I drop the ball and Watford score. It's easy to say what I should have done, but there's no need for an inquest. I made a mistake, simple as that. Before the match, we decide that at the end we would do a lap of honour to thank the fans for playing their part in an incredible season, but after that error I find it

The end of a long but enjoyable season.

hard to go around and wave. That's no disrespect to our supporters, but I just felt we hadn't done well today and maybe let them down a little. It's a disappointing way to finish our home programme.

May 10

I get a call from Bob Bradley, the United States coach, and he wants to know if I'm available for the Gold Cup and another tournament later in the summer. On the one hand I'm flattered to be asked, but on the other it was not what I expected and I'm not sure if I want to commit a whole off-season to international football. It's clear from what Bradley says, Kasey is going to play in the majority of

MAY 07

matches. He only needs another two or three to reach his century of caps and Tim Howard is going back to number two. I could use a break. I haven't had one for three years now and I'm ready for some golf. I don't see any point in joining the national squad just to be third choice. I ask the club what they think about it. They're not keen on me spending the summer over there. They want me to rest after a long domestic season and the World Cup before that and I know that if I ask to be released there will be some resistance. I think that if I knew I was going to be playing in these tournaments I might have put up more of a fight.

May 11

I ask Steve Sidwell where he's going at the end of the season, expecting him to brush me off in jest as he had done with all of us over the last few months. But he says, if you really want to know, I'll tell you. So he did. Chelsea. I'm pleased for him, but he's going to find it tough there. No question he's a good player, but I don't think he made as much of an impact in the Premier League as he did when we were in the Championship. He'll find a huge weight of expectation at Chelsea because they can't afford to lose a game. We wish him well, now that he has finally decided his future. The shame is the club gets nothing for developing him into a top flight player because he has reached the end of his contract, but that's the way it is nowadays. Sidwell was always consistent, even if he had a bad game by his standards it was still good by any other. There's no denying how instrumental he has been in our rise and we all acknowledge the huge part he played.

May 13

I'm not likely to forget this day in a hurry. We're at Blackburn for the final match of an incredible year and I break my hand. I knew from the moment Shabani Nonda clattered into me I had broken it. He also hit me on the head and when our physio Jon Fearn got out to me lying on the pitch he was more concerned about the blood coming out of my mouth, but I told him straight away my head was all right, but my right hand had been cracked. I was furious with

In agony at Blackburn.

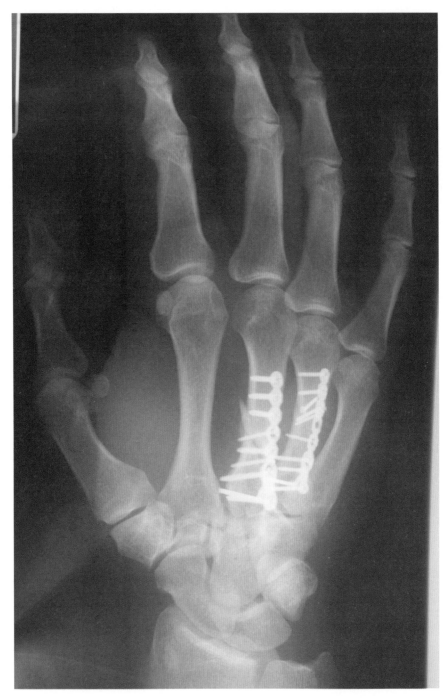

The X-Ray showing the 18 screws in my hand.

the referee. How was that not a foul? I was more concerned that the goal had been given than the injury.

After the break had been confirmed by x-rays at Blackburn hospital I waited until after the match to speak to the ref again and, while he was sorry I had been badly hurt, he felt Nonda had made a legitimate attempt to play the ball after I had left my line to reach the low cross at his feet. So that's the end of my golf for the summer and just about everything else and I can forget about playing for the United States.

The match was drawn 3-3. It turns out that if we had won we would have been in Europe. One more goal would have done it. Not that I had Europe on my mind as we travelled home. I just want to get my broken hand fixed.

May 14

I realise I'm going to need an operation to repair broken bones and the sooner the better. Jon Fearn says there's a hand surgeon in Windsor who can do something maybe on Friday, but that's not quick enough for me. I call my buddy, Mark Wiltshire, who works at the Steadman-Hawkins clinic in Colorado as a medical advisor, and email him my x-rays that night and he says: "When can you get here?" That's what I needed to hear. Through my connection I am on the plane as soon as possible.

May 16

I'm back in Colorado. I have a 90 minute operation under local anaesthetic to repair the bones joining my middle two fingers. The bones are pretty much shattered and in pieces. By the end of it I look like the Bionic Man with 18 screws and pins and two plates stuck in the hand, but it had to be done and now I have a long summer ahead of me when all I can do is hope it mends itself. I can't drive a car, water-ski, play golf or fly-fish, all of which I had planned to do. (I did actually take part in a golf day to raise funds for my old university later in the summer and went round one-handed).

If there's a good time to sustain such a bad injury it has to be the last match of the season, so to that extent I'm lucky, but I don't feel lucky and I spend too much time wondering if I'm going to be fit for the start of the next season in August. It's going to be close.

May 18

I hear Steve Coppell has been named League Managers' Association Manager of the Year for the second year in succession. It's deserved for what we have done under him over the last couple of years. I didn't notice any change of style or approach from him just because we were in the Premier League. He was just the same. What he has done is remarkable because he has some great players here at Reading and they remain underestimated. Nick Shorey, for one. He cost us £15,000 or whatever it was, and now there are people going for £6 million who are not nearly as good as him. And now he's going to be making his debut for England against Brazil at the end of the month. I reckoned he was unbelievable the season before in the Championship, him and Bobby Convey. Then Hunty comes from nowhere and does a fantastic job. That's one of the reasons Steve Coppell is so admired in the game.

May 19

Not long before the end of the season, I did some work for the Prince's Trust. They called the club and asked if one of us will go along and speak to a group of youths about being a pro footballer. These are kids for whom life has not gone well so far. This way, through the Prince's Trust, they get a second chance. Football is a way into them, a way of getting them involved. I was happy to go along and hang around with them for an hour and a half and answer a few questions. You could tell they love football and they really enjoyed a tour of the stadium. There was interest there and we overcame a few hurdles. In the end they gave me what must be a unique present, a football signed by them all.

May 20

I'm hearing from back in England how Sheffield United are fighting against their relegation. The Carlos Tevez affair seems to rumble on and I can't help feeling a little sorry for our old rivals. West Ham seem to have come out of it pretty well. To be fined £5.5 million is not much when staying in the Premiership is worth, what, £47 million to any club? If Tevez is owned by an agent and that's against the rules, why was he allowed to play the rest of the season?

May 21

Amanda writes.....

The season is over. We've had a great time and visited some wonderful stadiums such as Arsenal, Chelsea and Manchester United. I'm sorry we didn't get to Liverpool, that's for next season. Myself and the children go to all the home games and as many away as possible. The team have accomplished something special over the last couple of years. My lasting memory will be of Artur, Marcus's dad, who came over when he could to see his son play. Artur sacrificed a lot for Marcus, including promotions at work, to help him become a top goalkeeper. Marcus is aware of his debt to him and has dedicated his career to him in return. At the Newcastle match near the end of the season, when there was a great atmosphere in the Madejski Stadium and a big crowd, I turned to Artur alongside me and said: "Can you believe all this is happening?" And, do you know, just for a few seconds he couldn't say anything. He was choked. He's very proud of what Marcus has done with his life.

May 24

My mother and mother-in-law are commiserating with me over my injury and for just missing out on being the best goalkeeper, statistically, in the Premier League. David James pipped me to that accolade at the last game. Had I not been injured at Blackburn, I might have beaten him. To be second best out of 20 high class keepers is reward in itself and gives some sort of validity to what I am doing. It's a pay-off, of sorts. There are other Reading players high in the Actim Index, five in the top 100, which is incredible considering our humble background, but then, as I keep saying, we have some very good players. My stats show 247 saves, the most by any keeper, and 13 clean sheets in 38 games, which is remarkable and says so much about us as a defensive unit. I have some great guys in front of me.

May 30

It's going to be a long summer of inactivity. We're back in America, trying to do the best for my hand to heal itself, until the approach of pre-season training. Already I'm looking forward to another year in the Premier League. But then I've always looked forward to playing this wonderful game. I'm glad Dad made me play a sport and that I chose soccer. It has taken me all over the world and given me experiences I could only have dreamed about otherwise. I have played with and against some wonderful footballers. If Hunter and Austin take up football seriously one day, so be it, but neither Amanda nor I will push them. In the meantime, I've said it before and I'll say it again, I think I've cheated life.

Above: With the boys on our hike up Mount Rainer in summer 2007 – with my broken hand.
Below: Hunter, Austin, and their cousin Connor Day at a Seattle Mariners baseball game. We take the whole family group, around 20 people, every summer.

Friends from Colorado enjoying benefits from our beloved Vitamixer. From left to right: Kevin Fickes, Lauren Donaldson, myself and Frank Kohlenstein.

STATISTICAL APPENDICES

compiled by Jim Baldwin

Marcus Stephen Hahnemann

Birthplace: Seattle, USA
Date of birth: June 15th 1972

Season	Club	League App	League Shut Outs	Lge Cup App	Lge Cup Shut Outs	FA Cup App	FA Cup Shut Outs	Other App	Other Shut Outs
1997	Colorado Rapids	24+1							
1998	Colorado Rapids	28							
1999	Colorado Rapids	13							
	Total (MLS Lge)	**65+1**							
1999/00	Fulham	0	0	0	0	0	0	0	0
2000/01	Fulham	2	0	2	0	0	0	0	0
2001/02	Rochdale (loan)	5	4	0	0	0	0	2	1
2001/02	Reading (loan)	6	4	0	0	0	0	0	0
2002/03	Reading	41	18	1	0	2	1	2	0
2003/04	Reading	36	10	4	1	2	0	0	0
2004/05	Reading	46	19	2	1	3	1	0	0
2005/06	Reading	45	22	1+1	1	0	0	0	0
2006/07	Reading	38	13	0	0	0	0	0	0
	Total (England)	**219**	**90**	**10+1**	**3**	**7**	**2**	**4**	**1**

Summary (England)

		League App	League Shut Outs	Lge Cup App	Lge Cup Shut Outs	FA Cup App	FA Cup Shut Outs	Other App	Other Shut Outs
	Fulham	2	0	2	0	0	0	0	0
	Rochdale	5	4	0	0	0	0	2	1
	Reading	212	86	8+1	3	7	2	2	0
	Total	**219**	**90**	**10+1**	**3**	**7**	**2**	**4**	**1**

NOTES:

The Appearances column denotes full appearances + appearances as substitute.

The Shut Outs column denotes number of games where Marcus did not concede a goal.

The Other column includes LDV Trophy in 2001/02 and the Division One Play-Offs in 2002/03.

CLUB HONOURS

Coca Cola League Championship 2005/06

CAREER MILESTONES

100th Career League Appearance:
for Reading v Watford (a) on September 25th 2004 (Won 1-0)
200th Career League Appearance:
for Reading v Everton (h) on December 23rd 2006 (Lost 0-2)
100th Appearance for Reading in all competitions:
v Millwall (a) on August 28th 2004 (Lost 0-1)
100th League Appearance for Reading:
v Plymouth Argyle (a) on November 2nd 2004 (Drew 2-2)
200th Appearance for Reading in all competitions:
v Chelsea (h) on October 14th 2006 (Lost 0-1)
200th League Appearance for Reading:
v Manchester City (a) on February 3rd 2007 (Won 2-0)
200th Start for Reading in all competitions:
v Arsenal (h) on October 22nd 2006 (Lost 0-4)

Debut for Colorado Rapids
v Dallas 1997
Debut for Fulham
v Sheffield Wednesday (h) on April 16th 2001 (Drew 1-1)
Debut for Rochdale
v Rushden & Diamonds (h) on October 13th 2001 (Drew 0-0)
Debut for Reading (loan)
v Wigan Athletic (h) on December 22nd 2001 (Drew 1-1)
Debut for Reading (permanent)
v Burnley (h) on August 27th 2002 (Won 3-0)

Consecutive League Appearances:
89 for Reading between August 7th 2004 and April 15th 2006
when he missed the home game against Stoke City on April
17th; Graham Stack deputised.

STATISTICAL APPENDICES

Marcus was the only Reading player to appear in all of their 51 league and cup games during the 2004/05 season.

Most Consecutive Shut-Outs: 7 league games between October 29th 2002 to December 7th 2002

Marcus did not concede a goal in 757 minutes of league football from October 26th 2002 to December 14th 2002

Marcus has received 6 yellow cards during his career in England;
v Preston (a) on October 26th 2002,
v Leicester City (h) on January 28th 2003
v Millwall (a) on February 15th 2003
v Portsmouth (a) on April 21st 2003,
v Millwall (h) on November 15th 2003
and v Liverpool (h) on April 7th 2007

INTERNATIONAL HONOURS

USA - FULL INTERNATIONAL
Appearances: 6 Shut Outs: 1

v Trinidad & Tobago at Hasely Crawford Stadium, Port of Spain
on November 19th 1994 (Friendly) (Lost 0-1)
v Jamaica at National Stadium, Kingston
on November 22nd 1994 (Friendly) (Won 3-0)
v Honduras at Fullerton
on December 11th 1994 (Friendly) (Drew 1-1)
v New Zealand at Richmond, Virginia
on June 8th 2003 (Won 2-1)
v Cuba at Seattle
on July 7th 2005 (CONCAF Gold Cup) (Won 4-1)
v Guatemala at Guatemala City
on September 7th 2005 (World Cup Qualifying Round)
(Drew 0-0) (Marcus played the first half only)

Barclays Premier League Table
Season 2006/07

			HOME					AWAY					
		P	W	D	L	F	A	W	D	L	F	A	GD	Pts
1	Man Utd	38	15	2	2	46	12	13	3	3	37	15	56	89
2	Chelsea	38	12	7	0	37	11	12	4	3	27	13	40	83
3	Liverpool	38	14	4	1	39	7	6	4	9	18	20	30	68
4	Arsenal	38	12	6	1	43	16	7	5	7	20	19	28	68
5	Tottenham	38	12	3	4	34	22	5	6	8	23	32	3	60
6	Everton	38	11	4	4	33	17	4	9	6	19	19	16	58
7	Bolton	38	9	5	5	26	20	7	3	9	21	32	-5	56
8	**Reading**	**38**	**11**	**2**	**6**	**29**	**20**	**5**	**5**	**9**	**23**	**27**	**5**	**55**
9	Portsmouth	38	11	5	3	28	15	3	7	9	17	27	3	54
10	Blackburn	38	9	3	7	31	25	6	4	9	21	29	-2	52
11	Aston Villa	38	7	8	4	20	14	4	9	6	23	27	2	50
12	Middlesbrough	38	10	3	6	31	24	2	7	10	13	25	-5	46
13	Newcastle	38	7	7	5	23	20	4	3	12	15	27	-9	43
14	Man City	38	5	6	8	10	16	6	3	10	19	28	-15	42
15	West Ham	38	8	2	9	24	26	4	3	12	11	33	-24	41
16	Fulham	38	7	7	5	18	18	1	8	10	20	42	-22	39
17	Wigan Athletic	38	5	4	10	18	30	5	4	10	19	29	-22	38
18	Sheffield Utd	38	7	6	6	24	21	3	2	14	8	34	-23	38
19	Charlton	38	7	5	7	19	20	1	5	13	15	40	-26	34
20	Watford	38	3	9	7	19	25	2	4	13	10	34	-30	28

STATISTICAL APPENDICES

Reading Appearances and Goals

Season 2006/07

	Premier League		Carling Cup		FA Cup	
	Apps	Goals	Apps	Goals	Apps	Goals
Andre Bikey	7+8	0	2	1	4	0
Bobby Convey	8+1	0	0	0	3	0
Simon Cox	0	0	0	0	0+1	0
Ulysses de la Cruz	9	1	2	0	4	0
Kevin Doyle	28+4	13	0+1	0	1	0
Michael Duberry	8	0	0	0	0	0
Adam Federici	0+2	0	0	0	4	0
Scott Golbourne	0	0	0	0	1	0
Brynjar Gunnarsson	10+13	3	2	0	2	1
Marcus Hahnemann	38	0	0	0	0	0
Greg Halford	2+1	0	0	0	0	0
John Halls	0	0	2	0	0	0
James Harper	36+2	3	0+1	0	1	0
Stephen Hunt	28+7	4	2	0	0+1	0
Ivar Ingimarsson	38	2	1	0	3	0
Seol Ki-Hyeon	22+5	4	0	0	4	0
Dave Kitson	9+4	2	0	0	3+1	2
Leroy Lita	22+11	7	2	3	2+1	4
Glen Little	18+6	0	2	0	0+2	0
Shane Long	9+12	2	2	1	1	1
Peter Mate	0	0	1	1	0	0
Graeme Murty	23	0	0	0	1	0
Curtis Osano	0	0	0	0	0+1	0
John Oster	6+19	1	2	0	4	0
Alex Pearce	0	0	0	0	0+1	0
Nicky Shorey	37	1	0	0	2	0
Steve Sidwell	35	4	0	0	2	0
Sam Sodje	2+1	0	0+1	0	2+1	1
Ibrahima Sonko	23	1	0	0	0	0
Graham Stack	0	0	2	0	0	0
Own Goals	-	4	-	0	-	0

NB: The appearances columns denote full appearances + number of appearances as sub

Reading's first Premiership season

MATCH DETAILS 2006/07

BARCLAYS PREMIER LEAGUE

Saturday August 19th 2006
Reading (2)3 Middlesbrough (2)2
Reading (4-4-2): Hahnemann; Murty, Sonko, Ingimarsson, Shorey; Seol
(Gunnarsson 83), Sidwell, Harper, Convey (Hunt 83); Doyle, Kitson (Lita 45).
Subs Not Used: Stack, Oster.
Booked: Sidwell.
Goals: Kitson 43, Sidwell 44, Lita 55.
Middlesbrough (4-4-2): Schwarzer; Parnaby, Pogatetz, Riggott, Arca (Davies 45);
Morrison (Johnson 84), Boateng, Rochemback (Mendieta 68),
Downing; Viduka, Yakubu.
Subs Not Used: Turnbull, Maccarone.
Booked: Riggott, Rochemback, Boateng.
Goals: Downing 11, Yakubu 21.
Att: 23,855.
Ref: M Halsey (Lancashire).

Wednesday August 23rd 2006
Aston Villa (1)2 Reading (1)1
Aston Villa (4-3-3): Sorensen; Hughes, Ridgewell, Mellberg, Samuel
(Whittingham 59); McCann, Davis, Barry; Agbonlahor, Moore, Angel
Subs Not Used: Taylor, Laursen, Hendrie, Djemba-Djemba.
Booked: McCann, Samuel
Goals: Angel 34 pen, Barry 61.
Reading (4-4-2): Hahnemann; Murty, Sonko, Ingimarsson, Shorey; Seol, Sidwell,
Harper, Convey (Hunt 65); Doyle (Long 81), Lita (Gunnarsson 36).
Subs Not Used: Stack, Oster.
Booked: Ingimarsson.
Sent Off: Sonko (33).
Goals: Doyle 4.
Att: 37,329.
Ref: L Mason (Lancashire).

Saturday August 26th 2006
Wigan (1)1 Reading (0)0
Wigan (4-4-2): Kirkland; Boyce, Hall, De Zeeuw, Baines; Valencia, Scharner,
Landzaat (Kavanagh 78), McCulloch; Camara (Connolly 20), Heskey (Chimbonda 76).
Subs Not Used: Pollitt, Jackson.
Booked: Heskey, Scharner.
Goals: Heskey 38.

Reading (4-4-2): Hahnemann; Murty, Sodje, Ingimarsson, Shorey; Seol (Hunt 69),
Sidwell, Harper (Long 87), Convey (Oster 64); Doyle, Lita
Subs Not Used: Stack, Gunnarsson.
Booked: Seol, Sodje.
Att: 14,636.
Ref: M Riley (W Yorkshire).

Monday September 11th 2006
Reading (1)1 Man City (0)0
Reading (4-4-2): Hahnemann; Murty, Sonko, Ingimarsson, Shorey; Seol
(Gunnarsson 76), Sidwell, Harper, Convey; Doyle, Lita (Long 75)
Subs Not Used: Stack, Little, Hunt
Goals: Ingimarsson 23.
Man City (4-4-2): Weaver; Richards (Trabelsi 60), Dunne, Distin, Jordan; Sinclair,
Barton, Dabo, Reyna (Miller 73); Dickov (Samaras 60), Corradi.
Subs Not Used: Hart, Hamann.
Booked: Distin, Reyna, Sinclair, Barton.
Sent Off: Dabo (80).
Att: 24,092.
Ref: H Webb (S Yorkshire).

Saturday September 16th 2006
Sheff Utd (0)1 Reading (2)2
Sheff Utd (4-4-2): Bennett; Sommeil, Morgan, Bromby (Nade 88),
Unsworth (Gillespie 46); Ifill (Alan Quinn 46), Jagielka, Leigertwood,
Armstrong; Akinbiyi, Hulse.
Subs Not Used: Kozluk, Kazim-Richards.
Booked: Unsworth, Sommeil.
Goals: Hulse 61.
Reading (4-4-2): Hahnemann; Murty, Sonko, Ingimarsson, Shorey; Seol
(Gunnarsson 67), Sidwell, Harper, Convey (Hunt 72); Lita (Little 66), Doyle.
Subs Not Used: Stack, Long.
Booked: Little.
Goals: Doyle 1, Seol 25.
Att: 25,011.
Ref: A Marriner (W Midlands).

Saturday September 23rd 2006
Reading (0)1 Man Utd (0)1
Reading (4-4-2): Hahnemann; Murty (Bikey 89), Sonko, Ingimarsson, Shorey;
Seol (Hunt 85), Sidwell, Harper, Convey; Lita (Gunnarsson 76), Doyle.
Subs Not Used: Stack, Long.
Goals: Doyle 48 pen.
Man Utd (4-4-2): Van der Sar; Neville, Vidic, Ferdinand, Heinze (O'Shea 70);
Fletcher (Solskjaer 70), Carrick, Scholes, Richardson (Saha 58); Ronaldo, Rooney.
Subs Not Used: Kuszczak, Brown.
Goals: Ronaldo 73.
Att: 24,098.
Ref: P Walton (Northamptonshire).

Sunday October 1st 2006
West Ham (0)0 Reading (1)1
West Ham (4-4-2): Carroll; Spector, Dailly, Gabbidon, Konchesky; Benayoun, Mullins, Reo-Coker (Harewood 85), Etherington; Cole (Zamora 72), Tevez (Sheringham 71).
Subs Not Used: Green, Mascherano.
Booked: Cole, Carroll, Konchesky, Sheringham.
Reading (4-4-2): Hahnemann; de la Cruz, Sonko, Ingimarsson, Shorey; Seol (Hunt 79), Harper, Sidwell, Convey (Gunnarsson 77); Lita (Long 67), Doyle.
Subs Not Used: Stack, Bikey.
Booked: Seol, Long.
Goals: Seol 2.
Att: 34,872
Ref: U Rennie (S Yorkshire).

Saturday October 14th 2006
Reading (0)0 Chelsea (1)1
Reading (4-4-2): Hahnemann; Murty (Bikey 36), Sonko, Ingimarsson, Shorey; Seol (Little 64), Sidwell, Harper, Hunt; Lita (Long 73), Doyle.
Subs Not Used: Stack, Gunnarsson.
Booked: Ingimarsson, Sonko, Bikey.
Sent Off: Bikey (83).
Chelsea (4-3-3): Cech (Cudicini 5); Paulo Ferreira, Terry, Boulahrouz, Bridge; Mikel, Lampard, Essien; Robben (Kalou 82), Shevchenko (Joe Cole 63), Drogba.
Subs Not Used: Ricardo Carvalho, Wright-Phillips.
Booked: Mikel, Terry.
Sent Off: Mikel (62).
Goals: Ingimarsson 45 og.
Att: 24,025.
Ref: M Riley (W Yorkshire).

Sunday October 22nd 2006
Reading (0)0 Arsenal (2)4
Reading (4-4-2): Hahnemann; de la Cruz (Gunnarsson 46), Sonko, Ingimarsson, Shorey; Seol (Oster 77), Sidwell, Harper, Hunt; Long (Little 73), Doyle.
Subs Not Used: Stack, Lita.
Arsenal (4-4-2): Lehmann; Hoyte, Toure, Djourou, Gallas; Rosicky (Song Billong 77), Fabregas, Silva, Hleb (Adebayor 73); Van Persie (Walcott 73), Henry.
Subs Not Used: Almunia, Clichy.
Goals: Henry 1, 70 pen, Hleb 39, Van Persie 50.
Att: 24,004.
Ref: A Wiley (Staffordshire).

Saturday October 28th 2006
Portsmouth (1)3 Reading (0)1
Portsmouth (4-4-2): James; Johnson, Primus (Pamarot 46), Campbell, Stefanovic; O'Neil, Pedro Mendes, Davis, Taylor; Mwaruwari (LuaLua 72), Kanu (Cole 80).

Subs Not Used: Kiely, Kranjcar.
Goals: Gunnarsson 10 og, Kanu 52, Pedro Mendes 66.
Reading (4-4-2): Hahnemann; Gunnarsson, Sonko, Ingimarsson, Shorey; Seol (Oster 73), Harper, Sidwell, Convey (Lita 73); Doyle, Long (Little 55).
Subs Not Used: Federici, Bikey.
Goals: Doyle 84.
Att: 20,146
Ref: P Dowd (Staffordshire).

Saturday November 4th 2006
Liverpool (1)2 Reading (0)0
Liverpool (4-4-2): Reina; Finnan, Hyypia, Carragher, Riise; Pennant, Gerrard, Alonso, Zenden (Gonzalez 66); Kuyt (Fowler 87), Crouch (Sissoko 74).
Subs Not Used: Martin, Agger.
Goals: Kuyt 14, 73.
Reading (5-4-1): Hahnemann; Gunnarsson (Seol 80), Sodje (Bikey 69), Sonko, Ingimarsson, Shorey; Sidwell, Harper (Oster 88), Hunt, Little; Doyle.
Subs Not Used: Federici, Long.
Booked: Sidwell, Sodje.
Att: 43,741
Ref: U Rennie (S Yorkshire).

Sunday November 12th 2006
Reading (2)3 Tottenham (1)1
Reading (4-4-2): Hahnemann; Murty, Sonko, Ingimarsson, Shorey; Little (Gunnarsson 85), Sidwell, Harper, Hunt (Oster 80); Doyle, Seol (Lita 75).
Subs Not Used: Federici, Bikey.
Booked: Seol.
Goals: Shorey 38, Sidwell 45, Doyle 79.
Tottenham (4-4-2): Robinson; Young-Pyo Lee (Defoe 68), King, Dawson, Assou-Ekotto; Lennon, Zokora (Huddlestone 68), Jenas, Ghaly; Keane, Berbatov.
Subs Not Used: Cerny, Murphy, Ziegler.
Booked: Jenas.
Goals: Keane 24 pen.
Att: 24,110.
Ref: R Styles (Hampshire).

Saturday November 18th 2006
Reading (1)2 Charlton (0)0
Reading (4-4-2): Hahnemann; Murty, Sonko, Ingimarsson, Shorey; Little (Gunnarsson 88), Sidwell, Harper, Hunt; Seol (Oster 88), Doyle (Lita 75).
Subs Not Used: Federici, Bikey.
Goals: Seol 18, Doyle 72.
Charlton (4-4-2): Carson; Young, El Karkouri, Fortune, Hreidarsson; Rommedahl, Holland, Reid, Thomas (Ambrose 57); Darren Bent, Marcus Bent (Sam 79).
Subs Not Used: Andersen, Hughes, Ashton.
Booked: Fortune, Rommedahl, Hreidarsson.
Att: 24,093.
Ref: G Poll (Hertfordshire).

Saturday November 25th 2006
Fulham (0)0 Reading (1)1

Fulham (4-4-2): Niemi; Rosenior, Pearce, Knight, Queudrue (Bocanegra 45);
Radzinski (Routledge 75), Claus Jensen, Brown (Diop 75), Boa Morte; McBride, John.
Subs Not Used: Lastuvka, Helguson.
Sent Off: Pearce (16).
Reading (4-4-2): Hahnemann; Murty, Sonko, Ingimarsson, Shorey; Little (Oster 38),
Sidwell (Gunnarsson 33), Harper, Hunt; Seol (Lita 90), Doyle.
Subs Not Used: Federici, Bikey.
Booked: Harper, Ingimarsson, Sonko.
Goal: Doyle 17 (pen).
Att: 22,673
Ref: D Gallagher (Oxfordshire).

Saturday December 2nd 2006
Reading (1)1 Bolton (0)0

Reading (4-4-2): Hahnemann; Murty, Sonko, Ingimarsson, Shorey;
Oster (Gunnarsson 87), Sidwell, Harper, Hunt; Doyle, Seol (Lita 76).
Subs Not Used: Federici, Bikey, Long.
Goals: Doyle 33.
Bolton (4-4-2): Jaaskelainen; Hunt, Faye, Meite, Ben Haim (Pedersen 85); Davies,
Nolan, Giannakopoulos, Speed (Campo 60); Diouf (Vaz Te 60), Anelka.
Subs Not Used: Al Habsi, Tal.
Booked: Nolan, Ben Haim, Jaaskelainen.
Att: 23,556.
Ref: A Wiley (Staffordshire).

Wednesday December 6th 2006
Newcastle (1)3 Reading (2)2

Newcastle (4-4-2): Given; Solano, Taylor, Ramage, Babayaro; Milner, Butt, Emre,
N'Zogbia; Sibierski, Martins (Rossi 89).
Subs Not Used: Srnicek, Luque, Huntington, Pattison.
Booked: Solano.
Goals: Sibierski 23, Martins 57 pen, Emre 84.
Reading (4-4-2): Hahnemann; Murty (Bikey 90), Sonko, Ingimarsson, Shorey; Oster,
Sidwell, Harper, Hunt (Little 36); Doyle (Lita 81), Seol.
Subs Not Used: Federici, Gunnarsson.
Booked: Murty.
Goals: Harper 37, 42.
Att: 48,182
Ref: R Styles (Hampshire).

Saturday December 9th 2006
Watford (0)0 Reading (0)0

Watford (4-4-2): Lee; Chambers, DeMerit, Shittu, Stewart; Smith (Powell 84), Francis,
Bangura, Bouazza; Young, Henderson.
Subs Not Used: Chamberlain, Mariappa, Priskin, Spring.

Reading (4-4-2): Hahnemann; Bikey, Sonko, Ingimarsson, Shorey; Oster (Little 90),
Harper, Sidwell, Hunt; Lita (Long 75), Doyle.
Subs Not Used: Federici, Gunnarsson, Sodje.
Booked: Oster.
Att: 19,223
Ref: C Foy (Merseyside).

Saturday December 16th 2006
Reading (1)1 Blackburn (0)2

Reading (4-4-2): Hahnemann; Murty, Sonko, Ingimarsson, Shorey; Little (Oster 83),
Sidwell, Harper, Hunt (Long 88); Doyle, Seol (Lita 75).
Subs Not Used: Federici, Gunnarsson.
Booked: Murty.
Goals: Harper 41.
Blackburn (4-5-1): Friedel; Neill, Todd, Ooijer, Gray; Bentley, Kerimoglu, Savage,
Pedersen, McEveley (Nonda 46); McCarthy (Derbyshire 90).
Subs Not Used: Brown, Matteo, Peter.
Booked: McEveley, McCarthy.
Goals: McCarthy 64, Bentley 84.
Att: 23,074
Ref: G Poll (Hertfordshire).

Saturday December 23rd 2006
Reading (0)0 Everton (1)2

Reading (4-4-2): Hahnemann; Murty, Sonko, Ingimarsson, Shorey; Little, Sidwell,
Harper, Hunt (Oster 70); Doyle (Long 85), Seol (Lita 54).
Subs Not Used: Federici, Gunnarsson.
Everton (4-4-2): Howard; Neville, Yobo, Naysmith, Lescott; Osman, Carsley, Davies,
Arteta; Johnson, McFadden (Beattie 76).
Subs Not Used: Wright, Weir, Van der Meyde, Vaughan.
Goals: Johnson 14, McFadden 47.
Att: 24,053
Ref: S Tanner (Somerset).

Tuesday December 26th 2006
Chelsea (1)2 Reading (0)2

Chelsea (4-4-2): Hilario; Geremi (Mikel 70), Ferreira, Carvalho,
Bridge (Ashley Cole 70); Kalou, Essien, Ballack, Lampard;
Shevchenko (Wright-Phillips 58), Drogba.
Subs Not Used: Hedman, Diarra.
Booked: Ballack.
Goals: Drogba 38, 72.
Reading (4-5-1): Hahnemann; Murty, Ingimarsson, Sonko, Shorey;
Little, Sidwell, Harper, Gunnarsson, Doyle; Lita.
Subs Not Used: Federici, Hunt, Oster, Sodje, Seol.
Booked: Lita.
Goals: Lita 67, Essien 85 og.
Att: 41,885.
Ref: A Wiley (Staffordshire).

Saturday December 30th 2006
Man Utd (1)3 Reading (1)2
Man Utd (4-4-2): Van der Sar; Brown, Ferdinand, Silvestre, Heinze;
Ronaldo (Fletcher 78), O'Shea, Carrick, Park (Giggs 46);
Rooney (Richardson 79), Solskjaer.
Subs Not Used: Kuszczak, Saha.
Booked: Richardson.
Goals: Solskjaer 33, Ronaldo 59, 77.
Reading (5-4-1): Hahnemann; Murty (Sodje 59), Sonko, Ingimarsson, Gunnarsson,
Shorey; Little (Seol 66), Sidwell, Harper, Doyle (Hunt 73); Lita.
Subs Not Used: Federici, Oster.
Booked: Sodje, Gunnarsson.
Sent Off: Sodje (69).
Goals: Sonko 38, Lita 90.
Att: 75,910
Ref: M Dean (Wirral).

Monday January 1st 2007
Reading (4)6 West Ham (0)0
Reading (4-4-2): Hahnemann; Gunnarsson, Ingimarsson, Sonko (Bikey 54), Shorey;
Little (Oster 54), Sidwell, Harper (Seol 71), Hunt; Doyle, Lita.
Subs Not Used: Federici, Long.
Booked: Harper.
Goals: Gunnarsson 12, Hunt 15, Ferdinand 30 og, Doyle 36, 78, Lita 53.
West Ham (4-4-2): Green; Dailly, Ferdinand, Gabbidon, Konchesky;
Bowyer (Newton 19), Reo-Coker, Mullins, Benayoun (Cole 78);
Harewood (Spector 46), Zamora.
Subs Not Used: Carroll, Tevez.
Att: 24,073
Referee: L Mason (Lancashire).

Sunday January 14th 2007
Everton (0)1 Reading (1)1
Everton (4-4-2): Howard; Neville, Yobo, Lescott, Naysmith;
Van der Meyde (Beattie 71), Carsley, Cahill, Osman;
McFadden (Anichebe 46), Johnson.
Subs Not Used: Wright, Davies, Stubbs.
Booked: Cahill, Anichebe.
Goals: Johnson 81.
Reading (4-4-2): Hahnemann; de la Cruz, Sonko, Ingimarsson, Shorey;
Little, Sidwell, Harper, Hunt; Doyle (Long 38), Lita.
Subs Not Used: Federici, Oster, Sodje, Bikey.
Booked: Sonko, Hunt.
Goals: Lescott 28 og.
Att: 34,722.
Ref: M Riley (W Yorkshire).

Saturday January 20th 2007
Reading (1)3 Sheff Utd (0)1
Reading (4-4-2): Hahnemann; Murty, Sonko (Bikey 43), Ingimarsson, de la Cruz;
Little, Sidwell, Harper, Hunt (Convey 85); Lita, Long (Seol 73).
Subs Not Used: Federici, Oster.
Booked: Sidwell.
Goals: Long 44, de la Cruz 50, Hunt 70.
Sheff Utd (5-3-2): Kenny; Kozluk, Davis (Bromby 64), Lucketti, Geary (Gillespie 53),
Armstrong; Jagielka, Montgomery, Stephen Quinn; Stead (Nade 72), Hulse.
Subs Not Used: Gerrard, Alan Quinn.
Booked: Jagielka.
Sent Off: Gillespie (55).
Goals: Nade 77.
Att: 23,956
Referee: M Halsey (Lancashire).

Tuesday January 30th 2007
Reading (1)3 Wigan (1)2
Reading (4-4-2): Hahnemann; Murty, Ingimarsson, Bikey, Shorey; Little, Sidwell,
Harper, Hunt; Lita, Long (Kitson 80).
Subs Not Used: Federici, Oster, de la Cruz, Pearce.
Booked: Long.
Goals: Ingimarsson 31, Long 51, Lita 88.
Wigan (4-4-2): Kirkland; Taylor, Boyce, Unsworth (Jackson 69), Baines; Valencia,
Landzaat, Skoko, Folan; Heskey (Kilbane 58), McCulloch (Johansson 65).
Subs Not Used: Filan, Granqvist.
Booked: Folan.
Goals: Heskey 3, Landzaat 90.
Att: 21,954
Ref: S Bennett (Kent).

Saturday February 3rd 2007
Man City (0)0 Reading (0)2
Man City (3-5-2): Weaver (Isaksson 35); Richards, Dunne, Distin; Trabelsi, Beasley,
Dabo (Hamann 48), Barton, Ireland; Samaras (Sturridge 74), Vassell.
Subs Not Used: Jihai, Corradi.
Reading (4-4-2): Hahnemann; Murty, Bikey, Ingimarsson, Shorey; Harper, Sidwell,
Little (Oster 80), Hunt; Lita, Long (Kitson 75).
Subs Not Used: Federici, de la Cruz, Duberry.
Goals: Lita 79, 89.
Att: 38,676
Ref: H Webb (S Yorkshire).

Saturday February 10th 2007
Reading (1)2 Aston Villa (0)0
Reading (4-4-2): Hahnemann; Murty, Bikey, Ingimarsson, Shorey; Harper, Sidwell,
Little (Oster 77), Hunt; Lita, Long (Kitson 62)
Subs Not Used: Federici, de la Cruz, Duberry
Booked: Harper, Bikey
Goals: Sidwell 16, 90.

Aston Villa (4-4-2): Sorensen; Bardsley, Cahill, Mellberg, Barry; McCann, Petrov, Agbonlahor (Berger 75), Maloney; Carew, Young (Davis 88)
Subs Not Used: Taylor, Laursen, Ridgewell
Booked: Young
Att: 24,122
Ref: M Clattenburg (Tyne & Wear)

Saturday February 24th 2007
Middlesbrough (1)2 Reading (0)1
Middlesbrough (4-4-2): Schwarzer; Davies, Woodgate, Pogatetz, Taylor; Cattermole (Morrison 74), Boateng, Arca, Downing; Viduka, Yakubu (Lee 85).
Subs Not Used: Jones, Parnaby, Euell.
Booked: Taylor.
Goals: Viduka 7, Yakubu 69.
Reading (4-4-2): Hahnemann; Murty, Duberry, Ingimarsson, Shorey; Hunt (Oster 72), Sidwell, Harper, Little; Long (Kitson 62), Lita.
Subs Not Used: Federici, Gunnarsson, de la Cruz.
Booked: Ingimarsson.
Goals: Oster 87.
Att: 26,412
Ref: M Halsey (Lancashire).

Saturday March 3rd 2007
Arsenal (0)2 Reading (0)1
Arsenal (4-4-2): Lehmann; Djourou, Gallas, Silva, Clichy; Ljungberg (Diaby 70), Fabregas, Denilson, Hleb (Senderos 86); Walcott (Aliadiere 71), Julio Baptista.
Subs Not Used: Almunia, Traore.
Booked: Senderos.
Goals: Silva 51 pen, Julio Baptista 62.
Reading (4-4-2): Hahnemann; Murty, Ingimarsson, Bikey, Shorey; Little (Doyle 80), Sidwell, Harper (Gunnarsson 71), Hunt (Oster 65); Kitson, Lita.
Subs Not Used: Federici, Duberry.
Booked: Kitson.
Goals: Fabregas 87 og.
Att: 60,132
Ref: C Foy (Merseyside).

Saturday March 17th 2007
Reading (0)0 Portsmouth (0)0
Reading (4-4-2): Hahnemann; Murty, Duberry, Ingimarsson, Shorey; Little (Oster 84), Harper, Sidwell, Hunt (Halford 90); Lita (Doyle 76), Kitson.
Subs Not Used: Federici, Gunnarsson.
Booked: Duberry.
Portsmouth (4-4-2): James; Johnson, Campbell, Primus, Stefanovic; O'Neil, Mvuemba, Hughes, Kranjcar (Taylor 90); Mwaruwari, Kanu.
Subs Not Used: Ashdown, Traore, Cole, LuaLua.
Booked: Hughes.
Att: 24,087.
Ref: S Bennett (Kent).

Sunday April 1st 2007
Tottenham (1)1 Reading (0)0
Tottenham (4-4-2): Robinson; Chimbonda, Dawson, Rocha, Young-Pyo Lee; Lennon, Zokora, Jenas, Malbranque (Huddlestone 80); Berbatov, Keane (Defoe 75).
Subs Not Used: Cerny, Stalteri, Taarabt.
Booked: Rocha.
Goals: Keane 41 pen.
Reading (4-4-2): Hahnemann (Federici 46); Halford, Duberry, Ingimarsson, Shorey; Little (Oster 75), Harper, Sidwell, Hunt (Doyle 65); Lita, Kitson.
Subs Not Used: Bikey, Gunnarsson.
Att: 36,067
Ref: A Wiley (Staffordshire).

Saturday April 7th 2007
Reading (0)1 Liverpool (1)2
Reading (4-4-2): Hahnemann; Gunnarsson, Ingimarsson, Duberry (Bikey 46), Shorey; Oster (Lita 82), Sidwell, Harper, Hunt; Doyle, Kitson.
Subs Not Used: Federici, Long, Halford.
Booked: Kitson, Hahnemann.
Goals: Gunnarsson 47.
Liverpool (4-4-2): Reina; Finnan, Hyypia, Carragher, Arbeloa; Gerrard, Sissoko, Mascherano, Gonzalez (Riise 79); Crouch (Pennant 65), Bellamy (Kuyt 50).
Subs Not Used: Dudek, Agger.
Booked: Sissoko.
Goals: Arbeloa 15, Kuyt 86.
Att: 24,121.
Ref: P Walton (Northamptonshire).

Monday April 9th 2007
Charlton (0)0 Reading (0)0
Charlton (4-4-2): Carson; Young, El Karkouri, Diawara, Hreidarsson (Thatcher 24); Ambrose, Zheng, Song Billong (Lisbie 69), Thomas; Darren Bent, Marcus Bent (Holland 30).
Subs Not Used: Randolph, Rommedahl.
Booked: Song Billong.
Reading (4-4-2): Hahnemann; de la Cruz, Ingimarsson, Bikey, Shorey; Seol, Sidwell, Harper, Hunt; Long, Lita.
Subs Not Used: Federici, Gunnarsson, Doyle, Oster, Kitson.
Att: 26,271
Ref: G Poll (Hertfordshire).

Saturday April 14th 2007
Reading (1)1 Fulham (0)0
Reading (4-4-2): Hahnemann; de la Cruz, Bikey, Ingimarsson, Shorey; Seol (Oster 70), Gunnarsson, Harper, Hunt; Kitson (Long 70), Doyle.
Subs Not Used: Federici, Halford, Duberry.
Booked: Hunt, Shorey.
Goals: Hunt 15.

Fulham (4-4-2): Niemi; Rosenior, Pearce (Knight 25), Bocanegra, Queudrue; Routledge, Diop, Brown, Davies (Dempsey 68); Helguson (Montella 71), McBride.
Subs Not Used: Lastuvka, Radzinski.
Booked: Helguson.
Att: 24,082
Ref: L Mason (Lancashire).

Saturday April 21st 2007
Bolton (0)1 Reading (0)3
Bolton (4-3-3): Jaaskelainen; Hunt (Michalik 21), Ben Haim, Meite, Gardner; Nolan (Giannakopoulos 46), Speed, Teymourian; Davies, Anelka, Diouf (Thompson 31).
Subs Not Used: Walker, Martin.
Goals: Shorey 64 og.
Reading (4-4-2): Hahnemann; de la Cruz (Harper 74), Ingimarsson, Duberry, Shorey; Oster (Seol 73), Sidwell, Gunnarsson, Hunt; Doyle, Kitson (Long 77).
Subs Not Used: Federici, Bikey.
Booked: Shorey, Hunt.
Goals: Doyle 84 pen, 89, Hunt 90.
Att: 23,533
Ref: H Webb (S Yorkshire).

Monday April 30th 2007
Reading (0)1 Newcastle (0)0
Reading (4-4-2): Hahnemann; de la Cruz, Ingimarsson, Duberry, Shorey; Seol, Gunnarsson (Harper 90), Oster (Bikey 90), Hunt; Doyle, Kitson (Long 89).
Subs Not Used: Federici, Halford.
Booked: Hunt, Kitson.
Goals: Kitson 51.
Newcastle (4-4-2): Harper; Solano, Bramble, Taylor, Carr; Milner, Emre (N'Zogbia 60), Dyer, Sibierski (AmeMikel 54); Owen, Martins.
Subs Not Used: Srnicek, Onyewu, Carroll.
Att: 24,109
Ref: M Riley (W Yorkshire).

Saturday May 5th 2007
Reading (0)0 Watford (0)2
Reading (4-4-2): Hahnemann; Halford, Duberry, Ingimarsson, Shorey; Seol, Sidwell, Harper (Gunnarsson 79), Hunt (Oster 76); Lita, Kitson (Doyle 81).
Subs Not Used: Federici, Bikey.
Watford (4-4-2): Foster; Doyley, Shittu, Avinel (Mariappa 46), Powell; Williamson, Bangura, Rinaldi (Mahon 10), Smith; King, Henderson (Hoskins 82).
Subs Not Used: Lee, Priskin.
Booked: Avinel, Bangura.
Goals: Shittu 60, King 85.
Att: 23,294
Ref: D Gallagher (Oxfordshire).

Sunday May 13th 2007
Blackburn (1)3 Reading (1)3
Blackburn (4-4-2): Friedel; Emerton, Samba, Nelsen, Warnock; Bentley,
Kerimoglu (Dunn 69), Mokoena, Pedersen; Nonda (Derbyshire 66), McCarthy.
Subs Not Used: Brown, Henchoz, Treacy.
Booked: Samba, McCarthy.
Goals: McCarthy 21, Bentley 56, Derbyshire 67.
Reading (4-4-2): Hahnemann (Federici 23); de la Cruz, Duberry, Ingimarsson, Shorey;
Seol, Harper, Gunnarsson, Hunt (Oster 70); Long (Lita 66), Doyle.
Subs Not Used: Kitson, Bikey.
Goals: Seol 36, Doyle 58, Gunnarsson 77.
Att: 22,671
Ref: A Wiley (Staffordshire).

CARLING CUP

Tuesday September 19th 2006
Second Round
Reading (2)3 Darlington (2)3 (After Extra Time; Reading won 4-2 on penalties)
Reading (4-4-2): Stack; Halls (Harper 102), Bikey, Mate, de la Cruz; Little,
Gunnarsson, Oster, Hunt; Lita (Doyle 69), Long.
Subs Not Used: Hahnemann, Hayes, Osano.
Booked: Bikey.
Goals: Lita 31, 35, Mate 86.
Darlington (4-4-2): Stockdale; Duke, James, Holloway, Hutchinson (Close 89);
Johnson, Ngoma, Rowson, McLeod (Cummins 60);
Joachim, Carlos Logan (Wainwright 64).
Subs Not Used: Russell, Armstrong.
Sent Off: Duke (72).
Goals: Johnson 19 pen, Joachim 34, 52.
Att: 10,353
Ref: L Probert (Gloucestershire).

Wednesday October 25th 2006
Third Round
Liverpool (2)4 Reading (0)3
Liverpool (4-4-2): Reina; Peltier (Smith 74), Paletta, Agger, Warnock; Pennant,
Sissoko (Guthrie 62), Zenden, Riise (Kuyt 79); Fowler, Crouch.
Subs Not Used: Martin, Carragher.
Booked: Paletta.
Goals: Fowler 44, Riise 45, Paletta 50, Crouch 77.
Reading (4-4-2): Stack; de la Cruz, Bikey, Ingimarsson, Halls; Little,
Gunnarsson (Sodje 83), Oster, Hunt; Lita, Long.
Subs Not Used: Hahnemann, Hayes, Osano, Joseph-Dubois.
Booked: Little.
Goals: Bikey 75, Lita 81, Long 85.
Att: 42,445.
Ref: P Walton (Northamptonshire).

FA CUP

Tuesday January 9th 2007
Third Round
Reading (2)3 Burnley (0)2

Reading (4-4-2): Federici; de la Cruz, Sodje, Ingimarsson (Pearce 74), Golbourne; Seol, Oster, Bikey, Convey; Lita (Kitson 60), Long.
Subs Not Used: Hahnemann, Hunt, Harper.
Booked: Bikey.
Goals: Lita 27, Long 37, Sodje 55.

Burnley (4-4-2): Jensen; Thomas, McGreal, Foster, Harley; James O'Connor, Noel-Williams (Lafferty 70), McCann, Elliott (Garreth O'Connor 84); Jones (Mahon 70), Akinbiyi.
Subs Not Used: Branch, Spicer.
Booked: McGreal.
Goals: Akinbiyi 69, Garreth O'Connor 90.
Att: 11,514.
Ref: R Styles (Hampshire).

Saturday January 27th 2007
Fourth Round
Birmingham (0)2 Reading (2)3

Birmingham (4-4-2): Maik Taylor; N'Gotty (Danns 80), Martin Taylor, Upson, Sadler; Larsson, Johnson, Muamba (Kilkenny 80), McSheffrey; Jerome, Campbell (Bendtner 68).
Subs Not Used: Doyle, Nafti.
Booked: Upson.
Goals: Martin Taylor 47, Larsson 90.

Reading (4-4-2): Federici; Murty, Bikey, Sodje, de la Cruz; Seol, Harper (Osano 90), Oster, Convey; Lita, Kitson (Cox 78).
Subs Not Used: Hahnemann, Hunt, Ingimarsson.
Booked: Kitson, Federici, Harper, Bikey.
Goals: Kitson 3, Lita 41, 82.
Att: 20,041.
Ref: P Dowd (Staffordshire).

Saturday February 17th 2007
Fifth Round
Man Utd (1)1 Reading (0)1

Man Utd (4-4-2): Kuszczak; Brown, Vidic, Silvestre, Heinze (Evra 73); Ronaldo, Fletcher, Carrick, Park (Scholes 73); Saha, Solskjaer (Larsson 73).
Subs Not Used: Heaton, O'Shea.
Booked: Vidic.
Goals: Carrick 45.

Reading (5-4-1): Federici; de la Cruz, Bikey, Ingimarsson, Gunnarsson, Shorey; Seol (Little 89), Oster (Sodje 86), Sidwell, Convey (Hunt 71); Kitson.
Subs Not Used: Hahnemann, Lita.
Booked: Seol, Bikey.

Goals: Gunnarsson 67.
Att: 70,608
Ref: G Poll (Hertfordshire).

Tuesday February 27th 2007
Fifth Round Replay
Reading (1)2 Man Utd (3)3
Reading (5-3-2): Federici; de la Cruz, Gunnarsson, Bikey, Ingimarsson, Shorey;
Seol (Little 68), Sidwell, Oster; Kitson, Doyle (Lita 71).
Subs Not Used: Hahnemann, Hunt, Sodje.
Booked: de la Cruz, Bikey.
Goals: Kitson 23, Lita 84.
Man Utd (4-4-2): Van der Sar; Silvestre, Brown, Ferdinand, Heinze; Park, O'Shea,
Fletcher, Richardson; Saha (Rooney 76), Solskjaer (Ronaldo 89).
Subs Not Used: Kuszczak, Smith, Scholes.
Goals: Heinze 2, Saha 4, Solskjaer 6.
Att: 23,821
Ref: H Webb (S Yorkshire).